HOW TO MARKET

AND SELL

YOUR CRAFTS

From Making It To Making It Big
In The Crafts business

By
Gabriel and Kai Bandele

How to Market and Sell Your Crafts: From Making It, to Making It Big in the Crafts Business
by Gabriel and Kai Bandele

ISBN 1-882706-03-X

Library of Congress Catalog Card Number:92-97196

First Edition

First Printing: January 1993

Manufactured in the United States of America

Bandele Publications
P.O. Box 21540
Washington, D.C. 20009
(301)779-7530

Cover illustration by Michael Brown and Cheko Hall
Cover design and concept by Gabriel Bandele

HOW TO MARKET AND SELL YOUR CRAFTS:
From Making It, To Making It Big
In the Crafts Business

by Gabriel and Kai Bandele

TABLE OF CONTENTS

INTRODUCTION

Since the beginning of time, humankind has harbored a burning desire to create. This need to create was manifest in many forms, from rock painting in the dawn of civilization, to contemporary art and crafts in it's various mediums. Not even the advent of mass produced utilitarian goods and objects of beauty decreased this desire for handmade works. In fact, the onslaught of impersonal, mass produced items facing the market on a daily basis has made handcrafted items more popular than ever, constantly increasing the demand for quality handicrafts.

It is estimated that some 85 million people are engaged in creating some form of art or craft. Of these numbers, only 250,000 to 350,000 people create crafts professionally, leaving the field wide open. The possibilities for anyone interested in becoming a professional in the crafts business are very attractive.

Of all businesses, the selling your own crafts offers opportunities to a full range of people. Homemakers, hobbyist, the elderly, men, women, teenagers and children, handicapped or disabled and economically disadvantaged people; you can turn your creative endeavors into a viable business. The best part is, the start up cost are considerably lower than most businesses, the business can be based in your home, and if you are highly skilled, you can use a comparatively smaller time investment than many other business require. This business even offers opportunities for people with little or no business skills, and sometimes, even little or no prior craft skills.

Regardless of what your craft may be, from calligraphy to woodworking, the unprecedented demand for crafts in today marketplace, can carve your space in the market. This entrepreneurship can take you wherever your hard work, determination, and use of the basic business principles (which govern the crafts and all other businesses) will take you.

In this book you will find the keys to a successful crafts business, from making it, that is creating your crafts, to making it big, or finding great success. You will also find a wealth of business information, questionnaires to help you analyze and review your potential, and tips to help you make your business successful, so that however you choose to sell your work; regularly as a crafts professional, part-time, on weekends or seasonally only, you can turn your desire to create into a money making opportunity.

This book can change your life. It is based on years of trial and error, as well as proven business techniques that have been the foundation of business success for our family. We have been working for ourselves, in the crafts business, for over eight years, increasing in profitability as we go. When we started, we had no clear road maps to success. We offer this book to you so that you can achieve success sooner than we did!

The road to success is exciting. We hope this book sparks your creativity so that your journey can be as fun and informative as ours was, giving you the opportunities to grow and prosper professionally and personally that we were given. Enjoy your journey.

Gabriel and Kai Bandele

CHAPTER 1

THE CRAFTS MARKET

If you have a craft or crafts that you have developed to the degree that others would be willing to pay money for them, then you are ready to consider the crafts market. Even if you are a novice crafts person with no experience selling your crafts, or if you're only thinking of creating a craft to introduce to the marketplace, you will benefit greatly from examining the crafts market in general.

The crafts market, defined in it's most basic terms, is the demand for handcrafted products by the consumers that would most likely purchase these products. Fortunately for those who are interested in tapping into this market, the possibilities are virtually endless.

Because of the overwhelming numbers of mass produced items available, which cannot begin to produce those nuances that make handcrafted items so appealing, many people have become discontented and now look for alternatives to mainstream products. One would do well to consider the psychological principal that is the foundation of selling crafts; that people have a need to feel unique and distinctive and to own or give as gifts excellent quality items which reflect their individuality. This is basically what the crafts market is about; meeting this need for distinctiveness.

From functional pieces, such as handcrafted pottery, to wearable art or a simple pair of handcrafted earrings, it is evident that handcrafts have become a major force in the market-place. This observation is based on the growing interest in art fairs, crafts galleries, artist markets, and catalogs featuring handcrafted, limited production pieces, and the trend is increasing daily.

Once you understand the potential for success based on the tremendous market eager to buy crafts, it then becomes important for you to make a quality decision which will not only affect your own life, but the crafts market. The decision is this: will you sell your craft in the market place or not. This sounds deceptively simple, however, it is a decision of great magnitude, because daily, hobbyist and crafts people who have no real understanding of the crafts business expose their product to the public and through some common mistakes can damage the market for themselves and other crafts people, as well.

With the potential for this damage so great (and this book will show you how to avoid damaging the market), it very important to make this decision.

Before entering the marketplace, ask yourself:

1. Do I have the time to devote to being a professional crafts person? Consider your current occupation and whether you are willing to both work your job and be a crafts entrepreneur. Other considerations should be your obligation to your children, spouse or any other person with whom you devote a great deal of time and energy. Even if you sell your crafts on a part-time basis, it is still important for you to realize that in order to insure any lasting success, you must treat the endeavor as a business, with everything that entails.

2. How do I feel about accepting money for my work?

If you have any inhibitions about taking money or asking a fair price for your work, then you should definitely re-evaluate your decision to be a professional crafts person. Many crafts people love creating their product so much that they would be willing to work to cover the cost of the materials, only. Some will even waive that cost on occasion. This is definitely NOT good business for anyone involved (we'll show you why later in this chapter).

3. Am I willing to produce on a level consistent enough that I can meet the demands of my market. This includes having enough stock for crafts fairs, private showings, wholesale or consignments to stores and any other avenues for sales.

In this book we have included many questions to help you assess your goals, strengths and areas that need improvement. You will also find some questions repeated in difference contexts in other chapters. These three questions, however, answered before you consider your place in the crafts market any further, are the basis for a successful crafts business.

Marketing Your Crafts

With the interest in crafts at an all time high, it is much easier for a person to make a crafts business. The optimism present in the business twenty years ago (which put a flood of hobbyist in the market place) has given way to a more sound approach to marketing crafts and currently, not only is being a crafts person highly respected as a serious profession, there are more business resources and products than ever to nurture any crafters potential in this field and marketing expertise is more readily available than in any other time.

Marketing is a buzzword now so commonly used in

the business world that it has taken on almost mystical characteristics. Although it is discussed in hallowed tones, it is widely misunderstood. Marketing is simply every thing that you, the producer of the product, do to get your product into the hands of your customers. Not very esoteric, but certainly very useful in revealing the wide range of activities marketing includes. We will break the information down to it's most simple components and look at the most basic and useful aspects of marketing for the crafts person.

Production

Although some may disagree, We believe that production is the very beginning of marketing. Some people do not produce crafts for the market. This book, of course, would not be for them, but if you are seriously interested in selling your product (selling being an aspect of marketing, also), you will need to have a product with enough appeal to generate sales. You will also need a quality product, which exhibits excellent craftsmanship, excellent materials used in the work and attractive designs.

Once you have your product prepared to go into the marketplace, you must be capable of projecting whether or not you can produce enough merchandise to stay in business. This is one of the most valuable lessons in marketing. If you are unable to produce enough quantity to meet the demand for your product, you will find the door to your business quickly shut. This is true whether you create a market demand for your product or if a market for your products already exists.

Another consideration of production would be keeping a log of your time and materials used. Even the time you use to clean up your work area is included in production. This is covered in depth in chapter 4, the pricing chapter.

4

As you can imagine, production is a long, consuming process, even if you work fast. Production can sometimes be more than ninety percent of your work. Every consideration of production should be assessed in order to achieve success marketing your product. See, chapter 3, Making It, for more information.

Pricing

The next step to marketing your product is pricing your product. No matter where or how you plan to sell, the wrong price can make or break your business. You may be selling your work in a place where the market value is low because someone is under-selling a similar product. This may be fine, for the vendor doing the undercutting, but only for a season. When you ruin a market, it is ruined. When customers lose respect for a product because the seller places little value on it, that respect is hard to regain, and everyone else who sells a similar product is forced to lower their prices. Everyone loses, even the person under selling the competition. If you do your research, you can avoid this situation. You would have determined the value of the work, found out what people are willing to pay for it, and positioned yourself in a place where people are willing to pay what you will need to make money off of your product.

Even if you do undercut the market, there is a time and a place for that marketing strategy. You must always be sensitive to the needs of your fellow crafts entrepreneur.

Pricing does not have to be a big production. You can use some very simple formulas, but for all practical purposes, we recommend as thorough a system as you can manage without the process becoming tedious. The more precise and meticulous you are at deciding on your prices, the better for your business.

Factors such as your production time, materials, quantity, market trends, your reputation, the uniqueness of your product and the competition all affect your prices tremendously. The last thing you want is to do create a large amount of excellent work and price yourself below your worth and in the end losing money you may have thought you made. In this regard, pricing can be challenging, but it's not impossible to be able to decide the best prices for your work without a lot of complicated equations. For more information about pricing see chapter 4, Pricing Your Product Line.

Selling Your Product

When it comes to selling your crafts, the most important considerations are where you will sell and how you will sell. You may want to work on a very small scale, selling to select clientele, out of your own home, or even, not personally selling retail at all, focusing on wholesale markets and consignments in select galleries and stores. There is a wide range of avenues in which to sell your products, retail and otherwise. It's up to you to decide where, how and from whom do people buy your merchandise. The methods are as individual as the craft person.

One of the best aspects of selling your products retail, yourself, is that it's fun. This puts you right into the heart of the marketplace. It gives you, first hand, an idea of who is buying your merchandise and what their responses are to it. This experience is more valuable than any book you can read and deserves you highest consideration. For more information about selling your products, see chapter 8, Power Showings.

Advertising and Publicity

Advertising your business, is getting the word out! There are many creative ways of doing this, and some of them are very inexpensive. Good advertising doesn't mean you have to rent a bill board or make your name a household word, although these may be very effective! Advertising is using the media to promote your business (more about promoting later in this chapter).

Advertising methods to explore run the gamut from flyers to television. We find the print media, i.e newspapers, magazines, trade journals and newsletters, more effective than television and radio for the crafts person. There are exceptions to this, but not many.

Publicity is one of the best ways to advertise your business. Although publicity is officially supposed to be news, The wise crafts person is able to not only get publicity, but use it as an advertising tool, especially for promotions on the local level.

Publicity is the printing or radio or television coverage of your business, in the form of a news release or news story. Publicity gives instant credibility to your business, as people tend to believe what they read in the papers or see or hear on the television. Publicity is also cheap and considering it's impact, it is by far one of the most attractive tools to use to market your business. Publicity is not always easy to get, but there are ways to get it, making it essential to find out more about this valuable tool. For more information, see chapter 5, Simple Marketing Strategies.

Promotions

Promotions differ from advertising, although they can be closely related. Promotions are what you to do to make your product more attractive and accessible to the market. An example of a promotion would be a special sale. A demonstration of your craft in your studio, with a open house, is also a promotion. Any give-aways, lectures and appearances can be considered promotions. Advertising itself can be loosely considered a promotion.

As a crafts person, you don't have to spend a lot of money on promotions. For example, you may know that you will be participating in an art and craft fair. Often show promoters like crafters to demonstrate their craft. You can volunteer to do this, and send invitations to some of your best customers that say something like, "Kai Bandele will be demonstrating her traditional bead weaving techniques at the International Craft Expo, at the Washington Convention Center, Sunday September 1, at 1:00 pm. She will be exhibiting and selling her bead work in booth number 115." This could of course be jazzed up, but you get the picture.

This same copy could be used as a classified ad in a local paper's special events section. This could be idea, especially if you have a large rapport with your local market. From this example one can easily see how promotions and advertising are closely related.

Direct mail is also a good way to promote your business. This could be done a number of ways, including sending cards to your best customers, having mail order sales, and using a catalog to get sales. Direct mail can be surprisingly smooth operating, too. There is the basic information that has to be learned, but it can be most effective, with some products being easier to sell by mail than others. If you decide to do any publishing about your craft, i.e., you write an instruction booklet on a special technique or create a tool that makes executing your craft easier for crafts people, mail order is an ideal way to promote your business. For more about mail order see chapter 5, Simple Marketing Strategies.

The above factors are the basic essentials of marketing. There are innumerable variations on these themes, but these remain the heart and soul of successfully marketing your crafts. This chapter served to introduce you to the basic elements of marketing. In the following chapters, we will examine these areas in more detail.

When you have completed this book you should be well on your way to marketing your craft in a way that is effective, fun, and highly profitable, however, as I stated earlier, no book is as valuable as your own experience. This book is just a guide to success, a compilation of what worked best for our family, as well as other professionals in the business. Overall though, only your hard work and smart work will really pay off, but if we did it, so can you. Enjoy, and much success.

CHAPTER 2

THE CRAFTS BUSINESS

The crafts business offers many opportunities for the entrepreneur, but like any business, the crafts business is a business. Whether you want your business to be large or small, there are some basic skills that are vital to your success.

Being creative and talented, while these are certainly assets will not necessarily make your crafts business successful. Time and time again we see the image of the artist as an impoverished, tortured soul driven by passion to create. This image is inconsistent with the top crafts people who are making the most money from their crafts. The most successful artist or crafts person, is not always the most talented, but the one who takes care of business.

If you wish to make money from crafts, you must see the whole process, from idea to product into the hands of your customer, as a business. Just as order is necessary to be effective in practically every area of life, order is necessary in the crafts business. A business plan is vital. There is an old saying that goes "plan your work; then work your plan". Even in businesses that emphasize creativity this is true, perhaps more so, because of the subjective nature of the business.

Below is a listing of basics, in which you could use to

formulate a business plan. Whether you have just begun creating for the marketplace, or you are a seasoned pro, you would do well to evaluate these matters, and see where your business is in relation to them.

The Basics

In order for you to maximize your potential for success, these basic business principles should be implemented into your business and adhered to. They will be the foundation of your success as a craft person or for any business venture you wish to explore.

1. Define your goals and objectives. These must be very precise; any lack of clarity here could surely mean problems later. Update your goals and objectives periodically. As your business grows, you may find your interest changing direction. Although you will need to be consistent, a degree of flexibility in any business is desirable. Your periodic evaluations of your goals and objectives will provide you with parameters in which can chart your course, pulling back, or stretching beyond, as the business dictates.

2. Create a viable business plan. A business plan does not have to be elaborate. Basically what your business plan will do is serve to give you a specific course of action. You would have already defined your goals, and now you must be ready to go forward and make them a reality. Careful planning is in order, which will take defining the who, what, when, where, why, and how of your business. Be very specific about this, because ideally, what you have in your plan, is what you will execute. This is the ground work for your business activity. For instance, don't just say, I want to be selling my jewelry to museum shops, say rather, I want to sell my Jewelry to the Smithsonian Museum of African Art in September of 1994. Study, research and

consulting with other professionals in the field are key elements in creating a business plan. Put it all on paper, (or computer) study and refer to it often, make sure you are capable of meeting the demands you outline for yourself and then begin to make your dream happen. Again, be very specific. If you are vague in your business plan your actions will be vague and ineffective.

3. Define your product line. What is your product line? For this you need to ask yourself some penetrating questions:

A. Which of the crafts that I do, do I enjoy creating most? People usually do best what they enjoy most.

B. How do people respond to my work? Include friends, relatives and any objective parties. Expose your crafts to professional crafts people and buyers. Rate your craft with other crafts in the field by comparing your work to what you see in stores, galleries, craft magazine, and what you see in peoples homes or what they are wearing.

You will have to be objective, trying to see your work from the eyes of the market. Honesty with your self may be difficult, especially if you love your work and have a lot of support from family and friends. Remember the market is ruthless, and only a ruthless eye can determine if you can make it in the market.

C. Can I execute my crafts in a reasonable amount of time? Taking too long to produce any craft is counter productive, even if you love the work. Remember, you are going beyond your own satisfaction to production for the marketplace. If you create too slowly, unless you can quickly and easily sell your pieces for several thousand dollars, you will not have made a profitable use of your production time.

D. Can I produce enough quantities of my work to meet any market demands? You'll have to know both your potential and limitations. You'll also need to be able to project if you will need to hire people to assist you in some of the more mundane chores of your craft, like mixing clay or working with raw materials.

If your production time is better spent designing, assembling and a few other processes that only you can execute and someone else can do the less important work, can you afford to pay them? Would this extra expense be able to pay for itself in a reasonable amount of time. All these factors should be considered. Be as efficient, and economical with your business as possible.

E. Is there a demand large enough for my product to make it worthwhile for me to produce on a large scale? Depending on where you sell, the market can be very fickle. You may find little interest in your product, and then, with one well planned promotion or chance publicity, have a flood of interest in your work. Can you meet large demands? Are you willing to? Some crafts people are not willing to meet large market demands and thats fine, but you have to be clear about what level you want to take your business to.

The demand for your product is challenging to gauge. Although the crafts market is consistent, it does ebb and flow in the area of market preferences. It's possible to not have a large demand for your product and make a modest amount of money with a small, highly motivated market. In this case, you will need to again check your goals. If you want a larger market, is there one out there? Can you create one? Will it be worth the effort to do so?

F. If after reviewing these question and choosing my product line, am i able to consistently produce this product, and do excellent work? This question is very important. The burnout factor is very high if you've never produced volume before, and secondly, because you will need to know how much good quality work you can produce (just producing volume isn't enough if the volume is poorly executed). It is also good to consider what type of selling outlets are best for you based on your productivity in creating your best quality work.

4. Do you like paperwork? This business, like any other, creates paperwork that demands attention. This is especially important if you do retail shows, for this involves applications, deadlines, query letters, submitting slides and photo's, etc. There is also the matter of obtaining licenses for sales tax, vending licenses, business permits, registering your businesses name and more. Check your state and local government for information about what you need to do to operate a business, a consultant in the field can also supply you with this information, and possibly help you through some of the red-tape involved. A trip to your local Small Business Association office is also a good idea. Keep also in mind if you do mail order, postal regulations and permits. A visit to the local bulk mail center of the post office will be helpful in obtaining information about business mailings.

5. How does your product compare to the best in your field?
Remember that to make it in the crafts business it is not always important to be the best, but it is important to have skills, ideas or materials that distinguish your craft so people know that it is you, and you alone, that produces it.

These are basic principles that can head you in the right direction. Your study and inquiries will lead you to more specific information. Be unrelenting in finding resources that will help you run your business more effectively. It is even helpful to study business materials not directly related to the crafts business. Many business principles are standard in their approach, and studying them could provide you with some valuable insights about your own business.

In the back of this book is an appendix of valuable business resources for both the crafts business and general business. Study them, and anything else you can get your hands on. These things can be for your business a firm foundation on which you can build on for years to come.

CHAPTER 3

MAKING IT

Marketing begins with production, but what does production begin with? A plan. The wise crafts person understands that there a market for his or her product exist or will be created. With this in mind, production, with the market in mind, can begin.

Successful crafts business people create (produce) their merchandise with their business goal in mind. They "make it" with "making it big" in mind. This means that all of the elements that go into creating their products are streamlined to make the maximum, most profitable impact in the marketplace. This process entails in addition to working with your business plan (in writing), thoroughly analyzing your product before you expose it to the marketplace.

Is Your Product Ready for the Marketplace

As a craft person wishing to sell your product in a professional manner, your work should be of superior quality. It does not have to be complex. You may just create earrings out of twisted wire. Be it complex or simple, your craft should have a finished quality, without looking like it was fashioned in an assembly line manner and losing that "one of a kind" quality so important to crafts buyers.

In this business, the responses of friends, family and even other crafts people and professionals in the crafts business is vitally important. You will, however, need to know for yourself what makes a fine quality craft object. The following is a list of the basic components of any fine craft. There are other, more elusive qualities, but generally you can effectively judge your work by these criteria:

1. Excellence of materials used. These are the raw materials and components used in making your craft. Sterling silver, gold, porcelain, stoneware, cotton, antique beads, exotic woods; include the full range of materials. Is the material sturdy? Does it feel good, comfortable? Is it heavy or light? Does it draw heat? Does it attract or repel?. Is it toxic to work with or a common allergin? There are many questions you can ask depending on your craft. Be demanding of yourself and make sure you've covered as many possibilities as you can.

2. Excellence of craftsmanship. This is where you must be most comprehensive in assessing your work. Is it finished? Polished? Sewn? Are there any loose pieces? Have you done all that is necessary to complete it? Is it excellent work? Is your level of skill acceptable for the retail market? Friends can be supportive of your efforts; they know you. The retail market and buyer, however, must be ruthless. Do good, competitive work.

3. Excellence of design. Whether your work is traditional, unique or anything in between, your design quality will have to be a cut above the rest to do best in this business. That does not mean your work has to be complicated. Sometimes simplicity has great appeal. You will have to be aware of the best of what is traditional, as well as contemporary in the crafts business. Try to try to meet the needs of your market, while being true to your own forms. This sound difficult, but it is a necessary step to

18

insure the greatest success.

Of great importance, also, is your pricing. This is one area in which knowing your market is invaluable. If your market is of a higher income bracket and your work is available in exclusive locations only, your prices should reflect this. Consider not only what your market has the means of paying, but also what they are willing to pay or are comfortable paying. Bear in mind that if you price your work too inexpensively in some markets, it will not be deemed as valuable. On the other hand, you should not price yourself out of the market completely.

When deciding on the price of your work these factors are most important:

1. What materials were used in the work, and their costs.

2. How long it took you to learn the skills do the craft well.

3. How long it took to make the piece.

4. What the market price for similar work is.

5. If you travel from city to city to sell.
6. How booth fees factor into your costs.

7. If you are wholesaling or retailing.

These are some basic considerations for pricing. Chapter 4, Pricing Your Product Line, goes into greater detail about this important aspect of preparing your work for the marketplace.

A Crafter's Checklist

1. Have I used excellent quality raw materials and components in this work?

2. Have the materials I've used been tested for strength, durability, safety and toxicity?

3. Have I finished this work completely, leaving nothing more to be done to it?

4. Have I gotten a positive response for this work, from friends, family and peers?

5. Is the design of this work evocative, harmonious, and pleasing to the eye?

6. Does the work reflect the qualities that I am interested in conveying?

7. Does the work have a market, an appeal to enough people that it will be profitable for you to continue making it?

8. Does the work please me to do?

9. Can I produce large numbers of this type of work?

10. Is the work priced appropriate to the targeted market?

11. Have I groomed the work, and given it a proper presentation?

12. Do I have enough products to give a strong showing?

13. Do I have enough variety to have a reasonably wide appeal?

It is important for you to maintain your artistic integrity, however, it is also important to make your product accessible to the public. Don't make it so far out that only you and your select friends and fans can relate to it (disregard this if they are paying big money for your work). Versatility and business savvy is what's important here. Create your art and give it to the people in a palatable, affordable form. You can do both in a manner that is comfortable for you, while increasing your market appeal to support your more esoteric art work, having the increased cash flow to finance it.

CHAPTER 4

PRICING YOUR PRODUCT LINE

Pricing your work is a very important element in your business success. This is one area in which knowing your market is invaluable. If your market is of a higher income bracket and your work is available only in exclusive locations, then your prices should reflect not only what your market has the means of paying, but also what they are willing to and are comfortable with paying. This could mean, in some instances, charging higher prices if your market is uncomfortable buying products they feel are too "cheap". This often implies, whether it is true or not, that the products are inferior.

There many formulas for pricing. Some of the easiest are:

LOW PRICE = LOW PROFIT, HIGH VOLUME, simply meaning, if you keep your prices low you won't make such a high profit off your work, but you will sell more of it, or:

HIGH PRICE = HIGH PROFIT, LOW VOLUME, which implies selling your work at a higher price and making a higher profit off of each sale, but selling less.

Here are some other considerations for this approach:

1. What materials were used in the work and what are their costs?

2. How long did it take for you to learn the skill, do the craft well?

3. How long did it take to make the piece?

4. What is the market price for similar work?

5. Do you travel from city to city to sell your work?

6. Factor into your costs, this includes overhead, tools used, booth fees, etc.

7. Are you wholesaling or retailing your work?

This is a simplistic approach to pricing, always keeping in mind the competition. To the novice crafts person, this can be tricky, especially if the market is very competitive. The novice is often unaware of the nuances of the crafts market. It is possible to do well using these simple formulas, but we can't stress enough that this is a simple, trial and error type approach.

Now that we've gotten the easy formulas out of the way, lets look at some of the more involved pricing considerations. First of all, lets look at the two primary concerns in pricing your work:

1. Pricing too high can cause you to price your merchandise right out of the market.

2. Pricing too low can cause you to lose money. After your labor, materials, and overhead are taken into account, you may find you've worked for mere pennies worth of profit.

This is the foundation of understanding pricing. You can use any or all, pricing formulas, depending on your product line, but if you really want to bring a high level of business skill, as well as profitability to your business, then don't ignore these elements:

Environment

Pricing should reflect the environment the work is shown in. Exclusive locations can demand higher pricing. Even the other exclusive merchandise in the shop or show adds value to your work being there. In these instances, the pricing directs the consumers attention to the product's exclusive design and quality craftmanship. People within the higher income brackets tend to shop in exclusive shops with reputations built on selling items which reflect good taste and shrewd marketing skills.

Material's Value

The value of material is extremely important in pricing. A simple pair of beaded earrings could increase tremendously in value if the beads used are rare or antique. Even if someone gives you the materials used in your work, you must charge the value of them, or else you could damage your market, especially if your own supply is decreased. You would have then damaged your own business.

The raw materials used are not the only consideration. There is also the perceived value of the material in the market. An example of material's value is work crafted in gold. This type of work would usually be priced higher than comparable work in silver. This is because it is common knowledge that gold is more expensive than silver. A poorly executed piece, however, regardless of the expense of the materials used, will rarely sell more than a well executed piece constructed with a lesser quality material. Some pricing variables, however, are less apparent. Value differences work best when the value of the material is well known to the consumer, as well as the crafter.

Craftsmanship and Design

Exceptional craftsmanship will be prized by purchasers knowledgeable in the art and will be paid for accordingly. Excellence in skills to execute the piece, as well as originality in design dramatically influences the value of your work. This is especially important when dealing with sophisticated consumers and exclusive retail shop owners. In retail outlets such as art fairs and festivals where there is a greater mixture of consumers, this, while important, is less of a factor.

Reputation

A big-name crafts person can demand higher prices than unknown crafters. Winning show competitions, promoting your work and plenty of publicity gain a crafts person a good reputation in the business. Positive association with exclusive markets can also add to the perceived value of your product.

Essential Pricing Elements

Retail markup

If you plan to sell your product (wholesale) to retailers, who will expect to sell the work at a 50% markup at least, then you will want to price the pieces accordingly. Keep in mind that the markup has to be factored into the final selling price. If you sell your work on consignment, you can expect the seller to keep about 40%, however, since you own the merchandise, and have invested in the time and material involved in creating the pieces for consignment sale, an owning cost becomes part of the overhead. This should account for another 10% of the final selling price.

Materials and Labor

The costs here are direct. Direct cost are only about 20% of the retail cost. If you execute the designs yourself, you earn the labor portion of the direct cost, whereas, if you hire out labor to execute your designs, this portion is paid to the person who executes the design.

Note: Crafts people should always pay

themselves. This cost should be factored in BEFORE profit. A crafts person should keep very accurate records of his working time to properly be compensated for it.

Overhead

This comprises of a host of miscellaneous expenses, detailed in "Wholesale Pricing" in this chapter.

Selling Expense

This is comprised of the expenses incurred in placing your merchandise in retail shops. Even when you wholesale or place your merchandise on consignment you incur selling expenses. This would also include the commission for agents or sales representatives.

Profit

Profit, which should not include your hourly pay rate as the crafts person, consists of what remains as additional compensation you earn by managing the business. You may decide on 10% applied to the total costs as your profit or, on the basis of retail sales, 5%. With these figures in mind, your pricing can reflect this formula:

Materials + Labor + Overhead + Selling Expense + Profit = Price of Merchandise.

These are very important elements in pricing, which if not taken into consideration, can cause you to

experience problems in attempting to move from selling on a small scale on your own, to selling at larger volumes, mail order sales, retail shops, or even consignment. Successfully implementing these factors into your pricing considerations will give you more flexibility when expanding.

Counting Your Cost

There are basically two ways to base your pricing; on cost or on competition. Pricing on cost considers first and foremost what it cost you to make the pieces. It works from the bottom up starting from your cost to what the market prices are for the work. Competitive pricing considers first and foremost the competition, and then down to your actual cost. It works from the top down.

Pricing Based on Costs

1. Costs: When you base your pricing on cost, you are working from the bottom up. You figure the cost of the materials, an allowance for overhead and a set price that returns a profit for you. Keep in mind that prices you set to recover all your costs may not sell when competing with amateurs or crafts people who are unaware of all their actual costs. There is a delicate balance involved in succeeding in the marketplace. You may even consider using a consultant to help in this area.

Should you find your prices out of line, you have two options:

1. Increase your production rate.

2. Reduce your hourly rate.

Remember, expected hourly rate and production time are vital elements in pricing.

Competitive Pricing

Again, in pricing to compete, or from the top down, you begin with the work's final price and work backward. In this instance, the relationship between materials, production time, overhead, selling expense and profit still apply, however, in this pricing method, a major consideration is the market, and the more thorough an understanding one has of the market, the greater the possibilities of doing well with this method of pricing.

Wholesale Pricing

When pricing to wholesale, you can keep your method as simple as dividing the retail price in half so that the wholesaler buyer would have a 50% markup. This could work well for you, but not all wholesalers are interested in that price. Many buyers would like a higher mark-up, even if the mark up is by a relatively small margin.

It will take some experience to be able to sell your products well wholesale. Here are some important considerations to get you started or, if you are already wholesaling, to help you figure the best wholesale price range for your work:

1. Wholesale pricing should reflect materials, labor, overhead and profit. This should be true no matter what

price theory you subscribe to.

2. Wholesale prices depend largely on money allowed for time and overhead. Keep in mind that overhead should be kept to a minimum. This expense is the quickest way to drain you of time and money. For a detailed description of overhead see below.

3. Keep in mind that materials can be a relatively insignificant or a major expense. What is good about cost of materials is that it can be measured effectively. This is helpful in considering your wholesale price.

4. Note that if you price from the bottom up, pay yourself an hourly wage that represents what you feel your worth is with a fair return for your labor. If you price from the top down, pay yourself an hourly wage that adequately reflects your production rate.

5. Control your overhead. Overhead consist of all the costs or time consuming activities that come into play when producing crafts. This includes non-productive time such as clean up, travel and picking up materials time, time out for paying bills, office work and studying your art. Overhead can often be difficult to measure, however, it must be factored into your pricing, otherwise you will find that these elements diminish your earning power. Other elements of overhead include rent, utilities, sales expenses which include advertising, time in a store or phone time. There are also sales expenses incurred from paying your own sales help, agents, accountants (which are a must for a crafts people) and other miscellaneous expenses such as stolen or damaged merchandise, overdue accounts and petty cash expenses. Budgeting your time cannot be over-emphasized, especially in a competitive market. Keep overhead to it's bare minimum.

6. Remember that the store owner may not agree with what you feel the value of your work is. Don't fall into a trap of selling yourself too short. On the other hand, don't be so inflexible that you miss having a wholesale market altogether.

7. If your wholesale pricing seem to be out of line after you've considered these factors, consider increasing your production rate or reducing your hourly pay rate.

Studying the Market

Keep these factors in consideration in when you study the market for wholesale or retail.

1. You should study both the wholesale and retail markets.

2. Look for work that is similar to yours. Try to get as accurate a comparison as possible in design, materials used, quality and craftsmanship.

3. Always keep in mind the pricing principles mentioned earlier in the text. If you are working to get back the cost of your materials only, you will find

yourself quickly disillusioned. Remember, selling your crafts is a business, which works best with the basic laws of business in mind.

4. Keep in mind that hobbyist and amateurs, who are unaware of business principles, are a large part of the marketplace. They make it difficult to compete with simply because they underprice their work, do not pay themselves and basically are unaware of the business end of crafts work.

31

5.   Holidays, local craft shows, bazaars and retail consignment shops will attract most hobbyist and amateurs. One of the main problems with this kind of low end price competition is that the buyers in general do not understand the principles involved in determining the price and could possibly believe you are trying to rip them off. Overall, it's best to avoid such fiercely competitive situations, and focus rather on alternative routes of distributing your product, however, you may choose to adjust your prices during these seasons accordingly, just keep in mind that you could possibly damage your own market, once these events or seasons are over.

6.   Design originality gives you the edge over your competition because basically, no one sells goods directly comparable to yours.

7.   It is working smart to produce more work with excellent craftsmanship and charge higher prices, than to feed into producing lesser quality work at lower prices.

8. Use price "leaders". These are inexpensive pieces that generate interest in your work, which once having captured the attention of the potential market, you then have the potential to sell them other works at your normal price range.

9. Always work out intelligent pricing for your work. Do your homework. No serious crafts person would ever go into a potential store or market and ask the buyer, "What do you think I can get for these?" You are the one that knows what amount of time, energy and effort, materials, overhead, etc., goes into your pieces. Keep accurate records and study crafts trade publications for more descriptive methods of logging the elements that go into your work.

10.   Remember, overall your goal is to gain a fair

return, not necessarily increase your prices.

11. When competition forces prices downward, you can try to compensate by producing a product that is unique enough to rise above the competition, or you can choose to speed up quality production, by any means necessary.

12. If you sell your work to retailers, make sure that the price variables for your merchandise at each of the retail outlets are not too great, damaging your reputation and the wholesale market for your product. If a retailer sells your work to low, you may even want to discontinue selling to him or her, just to protect your market.

The art of pricing is very involved, and certainly outside the scope of this publication. As emphasized before in this chapter, study, do your homework, and keep good records.

CHAPTER 5

SIMPLE MARKETING STRATEGIES

In the first chapter we defined marketing as everything you do to take your product from production to the marketplace or rather, to the hands of customer. Chapter 1 laid a foundation which gave you an idea of marketing's most essential elements. We will now build upon those elements, further by elaborating on some of the elements already covered and bringing to light other marketing tools.

One aspect of marketing is that it gives a product visibility and, hopefully, attractiveness. It also encompasses tailoring that visibility to select individuals, targeting the greatest potential for sales, inquiries and interest in your craft.

There are several ways to market a product, some very elaborate, others simple and some even free. We will begin by giving some basic marketing tools:

The Business Card

The business card is a simple, but often overlooked marketing tool. Many times, a business card is the first and last thing a person will see about your business. For any craft person who wishes to sell his or her product on any level, a business card is a must. When choosing a design, keep these things in mind:

1. A professional quality logo distinguishes your card. If you are not graphically inclined, it is well worth your efforts to have an artist create a logo for you. Be sure it

represents your craft and evokes the kind of mood your company wants to convey, i.e country, cultural, high tech, sophisticated, etc. Keep in mind, also, the type of customers which you wish to attract.

Another option is to have a photo of yourself working on your craft, or of your product itself on your card. This, although more expensive, is very distinguishing. Remember, a customer is more likely to remember you if some element of your card jars his or her memory.

2.   Make sure the lettering on your card is fully readable.   Old english capitols, though graphically interesting, are a reader's nightmare. Be creative, but make sure from an objective party that the type is easy on the eyes.

3.   Don't use trite lettering styles or typefaces. Remember, you want to make a good impression. Make your card in even the simplest way, distinguishing.

4. Include all vital information: name, address, city, state, zip and telephone number with area code. Never leave off any of these, even if you have a p.o. box. This makes your card more likely to be added to important mailing lists and data bases, increasing your networking possibilities.

5. In a few brief words, summarize what you do, i.e.

Assata Nzinga, pottery, or Nefertiti Ra, illuminated calligraphy and papyrus accessories. Remember, descriptive and brief!

Building A Mailing List

In this business, having a good mailing list is vital.

Your mailing list can be used for anything from special promotions, sales, inviting customers to showings of your work or just special notes to keep you in the minds of your customers. Lists can be obtained from other businesses, friends, organizations, networks and list brokers, but the most effective and least expensive way to have a good list is to create your own. There are several ways to accomplish this:

1. If you are an itinerant vendor, collect the business cards of other crafters, promoters and people who buy your product at the shows you participate in.

2. Use a guest book to create a mailing list at all your shows.

3. Collect business cards from people who buy or show an interest in purchasing your product wholesale.

4. Collect flyers (with addresses) of people you wish to expose your product to.

5. Use the names of anyone who purchased any thing from you, or inquired about your business via mail order.

6. Take addresses off of checks you receive when customers purchase from your business.

Publicity

Using free publicity is one of the best deals around and free publicity, or rather air time or newspaper or magazine blurbs that are a direct result of press releases sent to the various media, give your business an air of credibility. Also, the air time or news or magazine coverage you get can be used to build your company more. This information can also be used in your own media kit.

Here are some of the most important elements of press releases:

1. Press releases must be newsworthy! Make them short, to the point, incorporating the 5 w's, who, what, when, where, and why and most of all, make them NEWSWORTHY. Stress and emphasize community benefits.

2. Try to have a good relationship to with your local editors, and media contacts. They are invaluable, but be considerate of their time.

3. If you cannot seem to get good results, consider having a professional public relations person draft your press releases and by all means, diligently study the art of P.R. and other press releases you see or hear.

Newsletters

We know of several people who have promoted their business effectively by using a newsletter as a tool to inform both customers and the trade and to advertise and promote their product, services, and related products and services. Creating a newsletter is highly effective, however, it is time consuming and can take a great deal of work. Also consider the time it will take to build up the circulation of the newsletter and the expenses such as mailing, printing, advertising, distribution, etc. If you do decide to pursue creating a newsletter, the rewards are many. Keep in mind, however, the main objectives of using a newsletter as a marketing tool:

1. To fulfill a need: perhaps for information, networking, suppliers, etc.

2. Promoting your craft: This is what it is all about if you wish to use your newsletter to market your business. You will want to garner an interest in your products and services in an informative, interesting, newsworthy manner. Stress benefits and make your work attractive and service and community oriented.

Create a Mailorder Catalog

Creating a mailorder catalog does not have to be a big deal. You can do anything from a one page flyer, folded into a brochure, a price list with photos, to a full color, glossy catalog, with several pages. The key here is effectiveness. You are aware of your market, or at least who you want your market to be. Try to meet the needs of your market, working within your budget, by presenting your work in a clear, comprehensive manner. A catalog differs from a brochure, in that it stresses the products you sell, rather than your business. A brochure would emphasize your business, a bio of you and your company, an explanation of your medium, etc. While a catalog can touch upon these things briefly, the emphasis is always placed on the product.

Some considerations for creating a catalog are:

1. Study catalog formats, collect catalogs you like and think you could reasonably produce for your business. Get estimates from printers and artists or factor in the amount of time and effort it would take for you to create it if you are doing the work yourself. Remember, research and development is the heart and soul of any business.

2. Factor in the viability of creating a catalog. Do

you have enough of a demand for your product to justify the expense? Will you sell or give away your catalog? Are you ready to do business through mail order? Can you meet the demand for your product alone, or will you have to have help with production?

3. What type of catalog is within your means to produce? Remember, you don't have to go hi-tech. You can have something simple, pleasing to the eye, clear and concise and be effective in your market as any full color, glossy. Even a photocopied catalog, on one sheet, if done properly, is perfectly acceptable. The most important thing is to do your research, and find out what other crafters have done in this area.

Brochures

As we mentioned in the catalog section, a brochure emphasizes not just the product, but the producer! Your brochure will give your business that "human touch", meaning it will give more information about you, how you started your business, and emphasize the benefits of purchasing your products and services.

A brochure is an excellent marketing tool because it goes beyond what your business card does for your business. It personalizes your image in the mind of customers and gives an overview of your entire business. It can create an ambiance for you, helping you target your market to a greater degree.

Your brochure's presentation should be as important as your bodily presentation. In many instances, your brochure will reach people who may never have an opportunity to see you personally. The image of your products and company conveyed in your brochure, therefore, plays a vital role in whether or not you turn a mere interest in your business into sales.

Here are some considerations for your brochure:

1. Decide on your emphasis. You? Your business? Your product? Ideally you should touch on all of these, but emphasize one. Build it up. Stress the benefits and positives attributes.

2. Study other brochures. Decide what you liked about them, what seemed boring or unnecessary to you, etc.

3. Use a picture of yourself, wearing your work, doing your work, or surrounded by your work.

4. Be personal. People want to know something about the creative process that produces your work.

5. Be brief. This is not an autobiography. Remember, you want your brochure to do a lot. It is your representative, preceding both you and your product, many times. Be economical in your descriptions.

6. Stress benefits and features. This can't be emphasized enough. Distinguish yourself. Make people want to buy your product, rather than buy the same product from someone else.

7. Do a excellent job. Brochures don't have to be glossy or full color, but they do have to be professionally done. This is not an area to skimp in. Even if you do it economically, do it well.

Wearing Your Product

If you create jewelry, clothing, or any other wearable art

form, wearing the products yourself can be one of the most dynamic ways of introducing your product. Nothing gives a customer a clearer picture of what your merchandise looks like "on". You can, if your merchandise lends to this, display a full range of your work, earrings, necklace, entire outfits. This shows your prospective market your versatility. You will also find that wearing your product generates a great deal of interest, leaving you an opportunity to network wherever you go, and to make, in many cases, some valuable contacts. Be sure to keep your business card handy when you are wearing your products, and most importantly, be positive and well groomed. You are trying to sell, and your personal appearance will be as influential to the overall effectiveness of you wearing your art as your work itself.

Displaying Your Work in Your Home

Just as wearing your art is a very effective way of displaying your product, so to is displaying your work in your home. Although the potential for exposure is considerably less, the impact to the chosen few to enter your home can be great. You can reserve these presentations to very serious buyers, store and gallery owners, or you can have an open house. Although there are factors to weigh in having an open house, it can be very profitable, with a low investment, should you choose that avenue. Go for a total image when you display in your home. Use your best work, and by all means take photographs. Feature your work in your home in a way that would appeal to your market. Your objective is to make your work appear to be easy to "live with". Any areas where you display in your home should be immaculate. Keep in mind also that the use of stands and display fixtures give your work greater dramatic appeal and impact.

Donate Your Product to a Visible Organization or Institution

This is a great way to get exposure for your work. The higher visibility and traffic the organization has, the greater your potential for building your market. The organizations and institutions could range from charities and schools, to restaurants, banks and offices.

There are several ways you can approach this. Often it is as simple as finding the appropriate contact person, donating the work and making sure you are given credit and that the people who view your work will have access to you for sales and inquiries. We must emphasize, in making a decision regarding who to donate to, use your discretion and make sure the process, although it is a donation, is somehow reciprocal. There is no a conflict involved in this. You are building your business, as well as giving to an organization or institution which you respect. Everyone wins. Be creative in your approach to this, even if you donate a piece to be used in a window display during a particular peak season, this can generate a lot of interest. A crafts consultant would be idea to use in helping you facilitate this process and to strategically choose the places you will donate to.

Lecture

Lecturing, like publicity, has the potential to give you instant credibility. One who lectures on a subject is generally viewed as an authority, whether they are or not. If you can present your ideas skillfully and be both informative and entertaining, you can begin to promote your work through lecturing. This is especially true if you have developed a technique or have an angle with which you approach your craft that would have wide appeal. Demonstrating your work also follows along the lines of lecturing, complementing your presentation. Although you can demonstrate at regular art and craft shows, outside of any kind of lecture circuit, demonstration your work during a lecture adds an interesting dynamic to your presentation.

Study as much material about lecturing as possible. Any good library should be able to supply a wealth of information in this regard. It is important when embarking upon a lecture that you practice, practice, practice! Never lecture sloppily or get before people not knowing what you are talking about. You will lose credibility and disrespect both yourself and your listeners.

Write a Book

This is easy to say, but not easy to do. There are a great number of factors involved in the process of writing a book and preparing to write a book often feels like creating a new career. The demands are great, but so are the rewards if you actually do it.

Writing lends an air of credibility that lecturing does not because it leaves your market with a tangible product. Although books can be derived from lecture series, books have much greater potential to propel your success because books go where you cannot and do not require your presence to sell. There are distribution networks that can sell your books at far more places than you could ever go to speak.

As a crafts person, your writing should address some need of your market. Instructional crafts books, i.e., book that teach more efficient techniques, etc. are good for crafts people. Also, something that generates interest in a specific product of your is effective. I know a doll maker who did a children's book about her signature doll, which of course did a great deal to boost the sale of her doll. She, through her publication, widened her market, and interest in her product line. I also know a woman who wrote an instructional book about using a popular material. Her book was very well received, especially by hobbyist and crafts people interested in using the material to expand their mediums. Again, be creative in how you approach this. You have a great deal of flexibility. Look at other publications in the field and related for ideas.

Be prepared to work hard. Writing a book is a full time job, but certainly rewarding and often, very profitable.

Teach a Class

Teaching is a simple approach to promoting your work. It incorporates lectures, demonstrating, working one on one with students and even writing on a small scale. There are many avenues in which to teach, i.e., local adult education centers, schools, from elementary to college levels, learning centers and recreation department centers. You could even teach out of your home or studio.

The pay is modest, but it does give you exposure and you can use teaching to get publicity, especially if you have a newsworthy hook to your teaching, such as, your classes are free to senior citizens, or you teach to handicapped children. These are very fulfilling ways to teach, especially if you love teaching, and of course, you are marketing your work at the same time. Remember, marketing includes not only selling. An important part of your work is getting interest in your product and exposure. Never ignore this process. This builds sales for the future and helps to ensure your crafts business longevity.

Promote a Show Featuring Your Product

When you promote your own show, you can get very

creative! You can go all out and do something outrageous or you can keep it simple and elegant. You can be brazen in promoting your work at your own show. This is one of the most fun and effective ways to market your work. Not only are you soliciting more customers and creating more interest in your work, you are also selling. You can't beat that combination.

Promoting your own show is not necessarily easy. You will have to decide upon the location, do all advertising and prepare the exhibit; in essence, you will do it all. That's not such a bad deal. Your maintaining control gives you a tremendous opportunity. Just make sure you do your homework. Don't throw your show together haphazardly.

If you do a show with someone else, make sure you have all the terms on paper. Miss no detail. The details in this situation, will mean your success.

Study any shows you attend (and do attend plenty of them). Keep a note book of the show's best features and the features you felt did not work as successfully, as well. Try to structure your own show with the best of what you've seen and experienced, but don't over do it.

Some further considerations for promoting a show are:

1. Have a theme and stick to it.

2. Within your theme, have a full range of work available.

3. Make available some accessory items if you can, as inexpensive fillers.

4. Make use of postcards and brochures, people who come to showings are most likely serious about art and crafts, and you want to leave them with materials to take

with them (in addition to any work that they buy) to keep yourself in their minds.

5. By all means, have a mailing list. This is vital for making potential sales later and for other mailings about your work and future shows.

6. Have all contracts in order, regarding everything; the space rental fee, insurance on your work, any terms you may have with other artist if it is a joint venture, etc. Put it ALL in writing.

7. Create a positive inviting atmosphere. You are trying to sell. Save your gloom and doom pieces for when you're famous. This is not to say that you cannot sell pieces with more serious themes. Just make sure the mood.

These are some simple marketing techniques. I'm sure that even reviewing them has given you some additional ideas. Always be open to the tremendous possibilities for selling and showing your craft. There should be no excuse for your not being able to generate at least half your income from your crafts, especially if they are well done. Opportunities abound.

CHAPTER 6

FINDING AND CREATING RETAIL OUTLETS

When it comes to finding (and creating) retail outlets, I like to think of there being two approaches, which I've named "the high road" and "the low road". The high road is the road that is most apparent. It is the conventual road, used by most, effective, relatively safe and sure.

The low road on the other hand, is not so certain. To take the low road requires quite often, a boldness of spirit and always creativity and industriousness. Both ways can be very profitable. Both ways involve some risk. Marketing and selling your crafts in the retail market should include taking at different times (and often simultaneously) both roads to finding and or creating retail outlets. Below is an overview of both roads and their risks and benefits:

The High Road

The high road, or conventional road to retail outlets includes any of the more conventional crafts markets. This would be the proven markets such as:

1. Art Fairs: Art fairs are specialty shows that can be as large as the biggest festivals, or smaller, community oriented events. The focus of art fairs is primarily visual arts, including crafts but there are some that emphasize arts such as music, writing and theater. Art fairs can be a solid foundation to build on, however, they are competitive, sometimes having dozens of artist and crafts people vying for a limited amount of space.

It's best to apply for these shows very earlier. Some of them have deadlines months in advance, and almost always, these shows are juried, requiring you to submit slides or photos of your work. Some shows also have a jury fee. This generally ranges from $10.00 to $25.00 and more often than not the fee is non-refundable. The specialized market of art fair attendees, however, will usually be sufficient to have a favorable showing. Target your market, well, and make sure your merchandise is appropriate for the consumer taste of the show attendants.

2. Craft Shows: Craft shows operate much like art fairs, but places the emphasis more on functional and decorative crafts. Craft shows are often smaller in scale, as well as participation than art fairs, but the buying climate is comparable. Crafts shows generally operate in the same manner as art fairs, having a juring of the artwork or craft, jury fee, early deadlines, etc. These shows can be very good, but again like art fairs, they are highly competitive and may be somewhat difficult for beginning crafts people to get into. Of course, there are smaller local crafts shows and crafts bazaars that are ideally suited to the beginning crafts person. These can take places in churches and social organizations, and usually have a low booth fee and small audience. They won't attract serious art buyers, usually, but they are pleasant and can give your craft work exposure.

4. Mall Shows: Mall shows are readily available markets. Usually sponsored by the mall itself, by promoters or by independent businesses, these shows can be found throughout the year (because they take place indoors, weather is not a problem) and are especially prevalent during the holiday seasons. These shows can be found by contacting the mall offices or watching for promoters who do these kind of shows often.

Depending on the mall, these shows can be very productive, having large attendances, but be aware, many times shoppers are not expecting a crafts show at the mall and are not prepared to purchase crafts impulsively and sometimes, mall shoppers even lack the time and/or interest in seeing a crafts show in a mall environment.

Mall shows are not completely awful, though. Since the crowds at a mall shows are generally generic (mall shows are notorious for improper advertising), they are more often than not successful (or else they would not be around). Have a good range of merchandise that appeals to the masses of shoppers and do a beautiful display. Remember you are not only competing with the other exhibitors, but the mall stores also.

4. Private Showings: Private showing can work nicely for you if you have the customer base that will support such an endeavor. This should include a mailing list of people who have a strong interest in your work and customers who have bought large purchases from you or several items at various times from you.

You have a great deal of flexibility in choosing the location of a private showing. Choices run the gamut from using your own home to renting a gallery space. Private showings can also be limited to very few customers or as many as the mailing list and customer base of wherever you do the show, i.e., a gallery, have available. These shows can be quite good for a crafts person, eliminating competition and a good deal of expenses (in some cases). The most important thing is to have a strong customer base.

If your support system is very strong, and your product has wide appeal, you may be invited by galleries to participate in a show. The financial arrangements vary, but you can generally look to pay a percentage of your sales. This type of show would usually include a reception and a longer showing, a week or more. These can be especially good to promote your work in the area you show in, as well as overall. Be sure to work on getting publicity for any private showing of your work, whether you promote it or not.

5. Home Shows: Home shows are very profitable for crafts people, especially if you are just starting out and for some reason cannot do the art fairs and craft shows. As with a private showing you can use your existing customer base, or if you are just starting out, you can have an open house, in which the public is invited. You will have to determine for yourself what kind of security risk this would be, but carefully marketing your open house can often eliminate many undesirable. Again, like a private showing, the competition is eliminated. Market your home show very carefully and be sure to get a mailing list for future showings, whether they be in your home or elsewhere.

6. Studio Shows: If you have a studio outside of your home that can accommodate a good number of people (about as many as you would have in your home at a home show), a studio show is ideal. A studio can be used as a small scale retail store in a way that would be inconvenient in your home. You can open your studio to the public or to your own customers on a walk in basis or for limited hours or days each week. This is especially effective if you have a large studio in which you can work, display your work effectively for retail sales and even demonstrate or teach.

One drawback to using your studio in this manner, however, is that you will have to be very focused in order to keep up your regular production schedule. No one can buy products you don't have, no matter how nice your studio is.

Another way to use your studio is by having a small showing, or open house. This would take less of a time commitment, especially if you like to use your studio for primarily for production. Operate this type of show just as you would an open house or private showing in your home, and be sure to create an environment conducive to retail sales. Your studio should be tidy, your displays should be creative and clever and most of all, especially if your craft requires the use of dangerous materials, your studio should be safe for anyone who visits it.

The Low Road

The low road, is the road less traveled. It is the road that offers as many offbeat, creative retail outlets as you can think of to do. The possibilities are as unlimited as your imagination. Some ideas are:

1.   Shows in specialty markets, restaurants, institutions,Corporate Shows, Shows in the offices of, or in conjunction with small, lesser known charities, etc: This is just a step a way from the high road, however, these, unlike the large art shows, craft shows and such, which are often saturated with competition, are a wide open market with fewer crafts people venturing into selling in these avenues. With a little work, and a lot of creativity (sometimes vise-versa) you can open many doors for retail outlets. Make sure you visit the places you're interested in showing at, and then decide upon a strategy to approach the appropriate people.   Be professional, have several samples, your brochure and any additional information about your product and work. You may, depending on the place you have in mind, have to contact the appropriate people by letter or phone. This is often the case, but sometimes just showing up, with a few samples and brochures, and introducing the idea is highly effective.   Be intuitive and thoroughly examine the potential market in advance. This will give you a better idea of who to approach and how to approach them to obtain the most favorable response.

2. Special Promotions: This could include home shows, but this allows you to really stretch out. Create

retail shows in a variety of creative ways, using a variety of locations and techniques for drawing customers. Have a crafts yard sale and sell your seconds, irregulars, and slightly damaged merchandise at a closeout price. Have also on hand, new pieces and plenty of cards and brochures. Not only would you generate cash flow, the overhead would be low, the profits high and the experience a lot of fun.

Have a show that features the work of special students that you have taught, this is especially effective if your students have needs that are apparent in the society in general, such as handicapped, elderly, homeless, and of course, sell your work there also. Any hook that would draw interest, widen your market, and have a strong possibilities for cash flow would be great. Target your timing. Don't always focus on the seasons in which crafts people and vendors selling are plentiful. You'll want to find any cracks in the retail market (that have potential) and fill them.

Create a notebook with promotion ideas. Be as detail oriented as possible, let the ideas flow, and refer to this notebook often, even if you don't do all the promotions you write about. This may spark some ideas that can enhance your other marketing efforts.

3. Use mailorder: You can do anything from a special brochure or catalog sale to a special promotion. Use your current mail list or buy or rent a new one. Here you have a lot of flexibility. What is important to remember is that unless you are using your own mailing list, the people who you target your mail to have never seen your merchandise. Good graphics and full color, glossy brochures are ideal, but if you cannot afford that, there are other quick and quality

color print methods available. The important thing is that you present your product in a manner that has excellent visual appeal. This is important even if the mailing is targeted to customers who are already familiar with your products.

As with any marketing technique, you will want to do your research, and by all means, for any mail promotion, stress the benefits of your product, no matter what product you have, or how eager your market is to buy, the benefits, clearly defined, help your customers feel good about their purchase.

Mail order marketing techniques are varied, and far beyond the scope of this book, however, here are some consideration for a crafts mailorder business:

A. A mailorder crafts item should be durable, lightweight, and easy to package and mail. Postage cost are considerable, so make sure your mail order product has a high enough markup to make it profitable.

B. Get as much information on the mail order business as possible. Even mail order techniques that have little to do with the product line you sell have much to teach you.

C. Be sure to visit your post office business mail center to find out which types of postal permits would best serve your business. They can also provide you with booklets about business mail, to help you understand the basic procedures for preparing your

mail.

D. Make sure you understand the mailorder business terms, i.e., direct mail, classified and space ads, etc. This will give you a clear picture of what would be most suitable for your product.

As with any other endeavor, you should thoroughly research the area you are interested in pursuing and talk with other experts in the field.

5. Custom Work: If you enjoy doing commissioned work and other related services like repairs, etc., custom work is for you. Custom work can involve you taking orders for special projects, doing large volume work, or repairing or consulting. Custom work is a good idea, regardless to your level of experience in the crafts business. You can use your custom work clients as references and of course, word of mouth and referrals from these customers can generate a tremendous amount of business. This is especially good for crafts people whose work may have some corporate appeal. One good, high paying assignment, can pave the way for many more jobs, which would be a great supplement to your shows.

Custom work can be demanding, though. You may have deadlines imposed upon you that are at times very unreasonable. Also, if the customer does not like your work, there may be some trouble collecting your payment. Always work out the terms well in advance and put everything in writing. Even if you do the work for friends, put the terms in writing. This will clarify matters if any problems arise.

5. Special Projects: Many crafts people can do well doing special projects. For example, I know of many painters who have done murals. These large scale projects did much to build the painters reputation in the community, while simultaneously increasing opportunities for publicity about their work, opening up new markets and other project opportunities.

You may not have a product line that would be

appropriate for these large scale projects, but perhaps there is another way you can get special projects. Lets say you make crafts for elderly people to enjoy at a home for the aged near the holidays. There are all kinds of opportunities available already and more that you can create. Brain storm and see what needs exist that you can meet with your crafts and how you can get the appropriate exposure and payment for your efforts. There are many possibilities, but you must possess the boldness to try them.

In conclusion, whether you take the high road, the low road, both roads or make more roads, the marketing potential for crafts, your craft in specific, is tremendous. Keep researching, experimenting and creating. There may be more people than you can even dream of ready to buy your product and from you! This does not even include your potential wholesale market. Just remember to explore all avenues, even if only mentally or on paper.

Retail markets, which generate a great deal of money, will be what you make of them. So, make sure you make the best of them.

CHAPTER 7

PLANNING A SUCCESSFUL SHOW

Successful shows are not just random happenings, even if it seems like it. For every effect there is a cause, and for every successful show there are definite ingredients that make up that success.

Retail shows are your opportunity to show your stuff! Have the right attitude, the right look and the right merchandise at the right show and you are guaranteed success.

This chapter will cover the basics of a planning a successful showing from choosing the right show to setting up your booth and display for maximum results. This chapter will also give you an idea of the work involved in doing a retail show. It's definitely more than it appears to the uninitiated to be, retail shows are one of the most dynamic, exciting aspects of the crafts business.

Choosing a Show

The question is not "is this a good show", it's more like "is this a good show for me". Choosing the right show is a subjective decision. Although some level risk is involved in any show you decide to participate in, there are ways to minimize the risks and narrow your choices to the shows that will bring you maximum results. This can be done in numerous ways. Common sense can often tell you if a show is good for your product line. Don't take your hand painted pork rinds to the gem and jewelry show in New York. You may do better at the piggly wiggly country craft bazaar (in fact, you may do best not taking your hand painted pork rinds anywhere). The point is, there is a show and a market for your product. It's up to you to find that market and supply them with what they want; your stuff!

In choosing a show the basic considerations apply:

1. Who is the market at this show. You can get customer profile from promoters, other vendors and people you know who have attended the show. Be as thorough as possible in gathering your information. What are these potential customers interest, tastes, spending habits, etc.

2. Consider your business plan. What place does this show have within the framework of your business plan. Will it promote your work in a way that has maximum impact. Can this show provide you with valuable contacts or expose you to a market that can increase your work's perceived value or will you depend on this show to provide cash flow. I don't recommend doing any show for cash flow only. Any show is a marketing opportunity, even if you have the misfortune to have chosen an inappropriate show.

These are a few of the areas that will need your consideration. Your business plan will dictate some of the shows it would be best for you to do. For instance, if you have in your business plan to have a country crafts store, you should focus on shows that will develop that market and attend as many show with country themes as possible. If you wish to have a contemporary crafts boutique in Soho, then you will need to develop a more exclusive, contemporary crafts clientele by doing shows that support that goal. Don't choose shows randomly. Even if you don't have a lot of information on the show, have some marketing tools on hand to make an impact, now or later.

3. Where does the show take place? If you have to travel to the show you will incur far more expenses than with a local show, and often when traveling, any mishaps

you encounter are far more difficult to correct. Local shows have their drawbacks too, however. It is often in your own area that the market, which can be the same from show to show in many cases, can grow tired of your style or your product line in general. You may even be taken for granted locally. Traveling exposes your work to a fresh new audience, whose appreciation pays off in dollars and cents. Here are some considerations if you do decide to travel:

1. What are the travel expenses involved: This would include hotel, gas, food, tolls, auto maintenance, and other miscellaneous expense. Keep in mind, also, the distances you will have to travel, and if you have the energy to travel that distance.

2. What are your expenses for the show. This would include booth fees, help, inventory, commissions, loss by theft or damaged merchandise, insurance, licenses, etc.

3. How has the event fared in the past. You can get this information from other vendors and promoters. It's true that you won't get the most objective opinions from promoters, but most promoters want vendors to be happy and do try to put on a good show. Just be aware and do your research.

4. Do I have the energy to travel and do a good show. This is very important. Your physical body can be worn out, just as an automobile can. A low energy level is a magnet for negativity. You are more prone to illness, mishaps, accidents, and people being unreceptive to you. If you are exhausted, it is better not to travel, you will need to be in your best form at shows you travel to and any loss you take at an out-of-town show, is so much greater than a loss you may take in-town.

Questions To Ask Promoters

61

As I mentioned earlier, promoters are not objective about their shows, but for the most part, you can glean accurate and important information about the show from them. Never abandon common sense, however, no matter what anyone says and always thoroughly research a show, as well as the city it will take place in and location, if possible.

Like a good reporter, you must find out what the five w's of this show are: who, what, when, where, and why. This would include getting information about the promoter. The nature and theme of the show, the show's date or dates, location(s), and the purpose of the show. The most important thing to remember is to get as much information as possible, in one phone call if possible.

It is a good idea to write down the information you find. You may even find it helpful to create a profile of shows you inquire about, even if you decide not to participate. This type of record keeping will always pay off when deciding upon your itinerary. It also provides references for other vendors who may ask what you know about certain events. Below is a list of question to ask promoters to help you choose wisely what shows you will participate in:

1. What kind of show is it? This simple question could mean success or failure for you at a show. Is the show for the trade, in which people will be interested in taking orders and buying your product wholesale? Is it a consumer show, which you will be selling retail directly to customers. It is also important to know what the theme of the show is. Does the show have a cultural theme, discount prices theme, personality or value centered theme. All of these consideration have an impact on customers. Keep in mind that anything that affects your customers influences their buying, whether positively or negatively.

2. Who is the market for this show? Get a complete customer profile. Most show promoters have the demographics for the show attendants. This type of information would include age, sex, geographic location, income, tastes, etc. It is essential to get as much information as possible. This is the one of the most important aspects to consider when choosing an event. It is also very important to find out the estimated attendance when considering the market.

3. Is the show local or regional, national, or international? Some shows are marketed only to local people, other show draw attendants from all over the country or the world, though presently their are not very many large scale international consumer shows. Keep in mind your goals for the show. For example, if you participate in a national retail consumer show with the primary goal of making as many sales (on the spot) as possible. You will need to decide how you can make use of the national contacts you will make, such as finding future wholesale clients or mail order customers for a catalog.

3. How does the show operate for customers? This information would include the show hours of operation, admission price and any registration processes. If the show is too much of a hassle to get into, this will discourage people from buying or even coming to a show.

4. Are there any other events associated with the show? This would include additional activities (with or without vendors) such as workshops, speakers, banquets, etc. When will these events take place in relation to the time in which the event you are participating in will take place? Will these events detract business away from you, or will they enhance business for you. If the events take place simultaneously, will they take place on the same level? What will customers have to go through to get from one area

to the other? How much time is allotted between events to allow for shopping?

5. What is the layout of the show? This is very important to know. The patterns of customer traffic make a great difference in how well you do in a show. Keep in mind that it is always a good idea to book a space early on to ensure you the best possible location. Corner booths, though in some shows are more expensive, are almost always high traffic and visibility areas. Find out if a map of the show layout is available for you to keep. These should always be kept with your show profiles for future reference.

6. What is the booth fee and what options are available? Many shows have just one booth size, usually 10 x 10, but there are shows that feature a variety of booth sizes and options. For example, for an additional charge you may choose to rent a covered booth, or tables, table coverings or electricity. You may also elect to rent multiple spaces. In this case, never feel inhibited about asking for a special rate for multiple booth rental. Also try to get a prime location and to have your spaces together.

7. What are the show's regulations? This information is usually included on the shows contract. This would include information about how booth areas should be kept clean, where exhibitors should park, load in times and locations and break down time, any special licenses or permits needed to participate, etc. Any special requirements needed should be considered. Remember, as a show participant you are an independent contractor. It is imperative to take care of your end of the business relationship.

8. Where does the show take place? This is important for you to know in order to prepare yourself

for both the market and the environment. For example if a show takes place outside, you will need to be prepared for inclement weather, including high winds. If a show takes place in an exclusive location, this may mean a more exclusive clientele. You should be prepared by grooming your image to appear more exclusive for this show. If a show takes place in a part of town in which there is a lot of crime, you should take whatever safety precautions as possible. Get as complete demographic information as possible.

Finally, always try to speak directly to a contact person for the show. This will ensure you the most efficient way to get the most accurate information. Try to get as much information in one inquiry (by telephone, fax, or mail) as possible.

Setting Goals

Once you have gathered the necessary information about a show, you are then ready to determine what your goals are for the show. This involves looking at your business plan and considering the data you collect about the show you are interested in. What is most important is that you match your product and goal to the show that would most likely generate the response you are seeking. Some common goals for participating in an event include:

1. Making sales--although this is the common reason most crafts people participate in a show, this is not the only consideration. Making those on the spot sales is only a part of what it is possible to achieve by doing crafts shows. Keep in mind that sales can encompasses direct and future sales and follow up for wholesale possibilities.

2. Introducing your product line to the public and to possible distributors, shop and gallery owners, etc.--In

making this one of your goals don't forget to utilize free publicity, consider doing a demonstration of your work or product and have plenty of promotional materials, brochures, card, catalogs, etc. available.

3. Meet customers--this gives you the opportunity to meet collectors of your work who may purchase through stores, galleries, or your catalog. This also gives you the opportunity to meet new customers and people who may not have purchased from you, but have a great interest in your work and who could become customers. Always be aware in doing a show at the customer's reactions to your work.

4. Build your Image--using shows is a great opportunity to do this. You can completely change how your work is viewed by your presentation of it in a show. Target your market carefully and then create through your display, attitude and promotional materials the image you wish to project.

5. Be aware of the competition--It is always wise to know where you stand in relation to the competition. This comparison should include your merchandise itself, prices, image, presentation, etc. Seeing the competition for yourself can help you creatively compete. It can keep you on your toes as well!

Remember that goals, like choosing an event, are very subjective. Your business and your business plan will best reveal what your goals should be. It is also important to rank your goals in order of importance. This will keep you reasonably focused.

Keep a record of your goals, their ranks and whether you have achieved them or not. Keep a record also, of to what degree those goals have been met. In measuring your goals, try to keep the process very simple. For example, if your goal is direct sales, your receipt book or inventory sheet can help you measure how many sales you made at a show. If your goal is getting new contacts, how many business cards you collect is the measure of that goal. If your goal is a new mailing list, how many names you collect in your mailing list book is the measure of that goal. What is most important to remember in respect to this is that you choose goals that are not vague or abstract so that you can measure them effectively.

Pre-Show Marketing

Pre-show marketing is a very effective way of boosting your sales in a show. There are many ways to accomplish this. Consider the following:

1. Direct Mail: This is highly effective for your existing customers. The more personal your mailing appears, the better. Consider handwriting some note cards to your best customers. Possibly consider renting a specialized mail list. This can be tricky. If it is a cold list you will have to try to determine the best way to use it. For example, say you know of an agency that has a list of crafts catalog buyers. If your show is in Atlanta, you may wish to send a direct mail package to the people on this list who live in the greater Atlanta area or the people who live in Georgia, South Carolina and Florida. For mail list rental information see your local telephone book for mailing services. As always, with any promotion stress the benefits of your products, have strong visual appeal and give complete information about the show you will be at. If you have a map, directions or a show layout this is even more effective.

2. Telemarketing: Customers love feeling that they have a personal relationship with you. Calling your select customers is a known drawing card for them. You can make

appointments for select customers to meet you at the show. You can offer them more specialized service while your assistant helps other customers. Even if you just announce you will be present at the show and give the show's location, time, etc., this extra marketing strategy is a high motivator for customers to come to the show. Often customers who respond to this not only come to the show, but they buy, even if it is a small item.

3. Magazine and Trade Journal Exposure: Often before large shows, craft magazines and trade journals will feature a section in the issue prior to the show about the event. Usually special advertising opportunities are offered in the issue. This is a prime opportunity to take advantage of exposure to gallery and store buyers who plan to attend the show. Take out as large a space as you can afford and be sure to mention your space number. Make sure also, to use graphics or photos that clearly represent your product line.

4. Press Releases: If you can get free publicity this would greatly boost interest in you and your work. The key here is to be newsworthy. If the release does not sound like news, it will probably not be printed. Make sure your press release mentions that you will be at the show and your booth number if possible.

5. Advertise in the Show Guide: People really do read these! There are business people as well as collectors that save these for future reference. Advertising here can also put you on mailing list that would be very valuable to you. Most important is the exposure to buyers that use these guides for reference. Buyers are always looking for fresh, new products. Make sure the ad you place represents your product and image well. Keep in mind also, the possibility to influence impulse purchases for consumers, just by having your ad strategically placed in the guide.

Planning your display

Crafts people have a tremendous range of display possibilities. One can use simple, readily available materials such as tables, a simple yet eye catching table covering, and one's merchandise to high-tech, expensive modular displays with wall panels, grids, shelves, lights and more.

Consider first what you have already. You can do a great deal with some simple supplies you may just have around the home, such as card tables, folding chairs and a plain colored table cloth.

Next consider what your budget is. This should not be done without a look at the marketplace and the competition. If the shows you plan to participate in require that you have the most high-tech display equipment then it may be worth while for you to invest in this kind of equipment. If on the other hand, the shows you are interested in have modest displays, then you will want to consider the basic equipment.

The many displays are well beyond the scope of this book but here are the primary display materials needed by most crafts people.

1. Tables--use strong and sturdy tables. Not the kind you buy at the general store which fold up and have practically no weight. Six foot tables are usually the best size. Heavy tables are worth the extra weight if it is to hold a lot of heavy merchandise, or if you need the stability against the elements at outdoor shows.

2. Shelving and racks--depending on what your craft is, these can be indispensable. Even if your product line doesn't demand crafts, additional levels make your display

more interesting visually.

3.   Glass display cases--use these for displaying special interest, fragile, or very expensive items that you don't want to be handled a lot.   If possible also have assorted sizes of glass displays, including some that can hang vertically.

4. Side and Back Wall Panels--these can have a grid pattern, be carpeted, velvet covered or wood. Most crafts people use these in their displays now. They offer wonderful possibilities for hanging your merchandise. They can also, depending on the configuration of your booth, give you booth a greater amount of space inside.

5.   Table coverings that extend to the ground--this gives a professional appearance.

6.   A sign with your companies name--many promoters provide signs for exhibitors and vendors but it is good to have your own sign also.   Use something visually appealing and easy to read that also conveys the image you wish to convey.

7.   A canopy or umbrella--These we recommend highly. In light rains canopies can keep your booth open. They also give your space greater visibility because any covered space draws more attention than and other space. Canopies and umbrellas, among their many advantages, also protect you from the elements, not just rain but sun and mild winds. Note: canopies are not buildings. They will not hold up against heavy downpours or extremely high winds.

These items are basics for display. Crafts people with a heavy show schedule need far more equipment than this. For a complete listing of equipment suppliers see the resource section in the Appendix (?) section at the end of this book.

With the equipment you have in mind, consider what your goals are for your display. A good rule to remember is that displays should do what is commonly known in advertising books as A.I.D.A., which is A--attract attention, I--build Interest, D--create Desire, and A--demand Action. If the booth and display draws attention, customers would be inclined to take interest, if then they come to the booth and are interested, then you want to convey through your display the desire to own your product. If the customer then desires your product, you can then compel them to act, or buy your work. This process can be done in several ways. It just takes creativity.

It is also very important to go to look at other crafts people's displays. This keeps you aware of what the competition is using. The public's response and current display trends in the business. Take the best of what you see and try to implement what is appropriate to your own display. Be careful not to over do it. More is not always better.

Preparing for the Show

In order to properly prepare for a show there are some basic considerations that you should address. After you have decided on the goals you have in mind for the show, you will then need to do the following:

1. Make sure you have enough stock. It is rarely a good marketing strategy to appear at a show with a small amount of stock. Even if the show has a small estimated attendance. Selling out of your merchandise is great, that is if you had enough of it from the start. Ideally you should have on hand at all time enough stock to do two or three

strong showings. This will provide you with enough stock on hand should any opportunities arise unexpectantly. This would also be good to have if you can have someone sell for you at other shows. You could sell at one show while the other person sells simultaneously at another show.

2. Pack your stock in an orderly fashion, insuring the least possibility for damage. We like to use large plastic bins with lids. These bins come in assorted sizes and stack on top of each other. These are excellent for travel. These bins can also be labeled to indicate their contents.

Depending on the type of merchandise you have, plastic bins, such as the ones just described may not be appropriate. If you are new to the businesses and are unsure about how to pack your merchandise you can ask someone with similar merchandise how they pack and prepare it for a show. This should be done in your preliminary research. If on the other hand, you are a seasoned crafts person, stick with what experience has taught you is best. Always keep in mind, however, improvements that may be made on your current system.

3. Make sure you take all the necessary small items that are useful at a show. These items include mirrors, charge slips and the credit card processing machine (if applicable), ink pens, business cards, brochures, price tags, signage (if applicable), and also any addition equipment such as rope, tools to assemble your display, etc..

4. Have your items priced and primed. By primed I mean have the merchandise ready for it's best presentation. It should be polished, finished, have fresh tags, clean and ready for the market. Pricing your merchandise makes it easier on your customer. Some people are inhibited about asking the price of items.

Each individual will develop a system for preparing

for a show. It is best to have a system that is methodical and comprehensive. This kind of organization will ensure a smooth transition to the show.

Setting Up

Setting up is the process of preparing your booth or space for your presentation and selling. This includes the loading in of your merchandise, preparing your display, and putting all superfluous items away.

Loading in

Use a common-sense when approach when loading in your merchandise. The first thing you will need to know is where the loading in takes place and what time. Knowing what time to load in can help you avoid vendor traffic and having your vehicle blocked in. It is usually best to arrive early.
Arriving late can be advantageous because most vendors have already set up. In this situation, however, the advantageous usually do not outweigh the disadvantages.

Make sure your merchandise is safe when loading in. There are people who know this is a vulnerable time for vendors. Many thefts take place at this time. We know of a vendor who was robbed at gunpoint early in the morning while loading in before a flea market showing. It's is always best to use common sense and basic safety habits when approaching any loading in and
breaking down.

One way to operate your loading in is to use your assistant (if you have one) to watch the merchandise at the booth as you bring it. They can also begin setting up the display equipment and organizing the boxes or bins of merchandise according to where they will be displayed. This saves time and energy. Make sure the merchandise in your vehicle is safe during this process.

If you don't have an assistant you can ask another vendor to help you by watching your merchandise as you bring it in. If you have to do this, still use caution. Try to set up your tables first and put your boxes of merchandise under the table as you load in. Always keep the merchandise consolidated rather than scattered haphazardly in your space if you are alone.

Once you have loaded all your merchandise and have arranged it in an orderly fashion, you are then ready to set up.

Set Up

Set up is a term that describes assembling your display and preparing your entire booth for sales. Your set up time has a lot to do with the type of equipment and merchandise you have. If you have an elaborate display, complete with canopy, shelving and signs that involve a great deal of assembly, then you should count on arriving early to have plenty of time. Many shows even allow setting up the evening before the show. This could be very advantageous if you have a very labor intensive set up.

It is best to arrive early at a set up. You are less likely to be moved if there is a space discrepancy, and the sooner you are set up, the sooner you can sell. We have sold hundreds of dollars worth of merchandise sometimes before a show was officially open. Sometimes to show volunteers and other vendors! Also, if you arrive early enough, you may find a clear space that could accommodate your booth that may be better than the space you are in. I've done this often, and we have never been disappointed with the results.

Approach setting up your booth methodically. We find it best to set up canopy first, then tables, table coverings, shelving and levels, then merchandise. According to what equipment you have this may work a bit differently. Our point is to make sure you are not creating more work for your self. For example, we have the kind of canopies that require no assembly and can be set up in minutes through what is basically one pulling maneuver. If we set up our tables first, and then your canopy, we would have to move the tables aside to get the canopy around them. This would be a waste of time and energy. A rule of thumb is to work in a manner that will prepare you for selling as quickly as possible. If you arrange your set up so that a section is ready for selling when you finish it, you can make money from that one section while you are still setting up.

When displaying your merchandise keep in mind the concept of A.I.D.A, (see above "Planning Your Display). Remember, you will be operating in very little space. It is very important to maximize your impact on potential customers. This should be done as efficiently as possible.

Consider the following in creating your display:

1. Have maximum impact: Ideally you should generate attention and interest, while simultaneously conveying an image that your market would relate to and feel positive about. This image should somehow imply directly or indirectly the benefits of having your products. Next of course, is compelling the potential customers to buy. Be as efficient as possible in carrying out these ideas.

2. Have an positive image: Whether it is on purpose or not, your booth and display portray an image of you. It is best to create your image purposely. Everything you use in your display, including your merchandise convey your image. Make sure your image is harmonious. For example,

don't mix country with art deco. You don't have to have one theme, but if you mix your themes make sure the blend is tasteful.

3.   Use design principles: It is a good idea to familiarize yourself with some basic design principles. This can be done by simply visiting your local library and reading through some design books.   Look for information about color, texture, creating illusions, levels, etc.   If you arrive early enough, you can experiment with different ideas.

4.   Keep in mind lighting in any display that you have.   Electricity almost always cost more, and can often limit your choice of available space. We like to do without lighting if possible, but we do have lights and heavy-duty long extension cords.   There have been times in which lighting was essential. Try to anticipate whatever you may need, while keeping simplicity and economy the focus of your display.

5. Pack empty bins, boxes and containers neatly and out of sight. Remember in setting up your display to leave a place for miscellaneous objects

which will be useful during the show such as business cards, a file for new contacts, brochures, ink pens, charge slips, etc. These items should be accessible so that you do not have to take your attention away from the customer at anytime. Also have a place out of view for personal items such as briefcases, purses, coats, etc.

6. Reinforce your business name: This can be done with various graphical elements. Signs, brochures, even t-shirts with your artwork and business name can be effective. This marketing technique puts your name and/or product visually in the minds of your market. The stronger the image, the more likely it is to be remembered. When

customers remember you, they are more likely to come back to your booth, recommend your booth or buy from you later.

7. Make sure your products are not obstructing each other. Smaller items should be placed in the front of your display, while larger items should go in the back. Also keep in mind positioning certain items for impulse sales. The area where you finish your sales transactions is good for this. Considering using point of purchase sale items such as gift boxes, note card, etc.

The information covered in this chapter is just for preparation for the show! This clearly indicates the work involved in this business. The rewards are great, however, and the fun is yet to come!

CHAPTER 8

POWER SHOWINGS

Once you have diligently prepared for a show, you are ready to make some money! This is the fun part. This is when you get right there in the marketplace for yourself, experiencing the joy, ego boost, frustrations and at the end of the day, probably fatigue.

Yes, shows are challenging but they are one of the most effective avenues to market your crafts available. At a retail show, you can make some marketing power moves. This chapter will outline how to make the most out of the time that you are actually showing.

Selling

There are volumes of work on selling. Rather than be redundant, we will outline the basic of selling, which you can personalize to your own style. If you are a novice in the marketplace, you can stay within these guide lines and develop your own style. Experience is most valuable here. As you interact in the marketplace you will begin to be aware of the subtleties that mean the difference between a sale and no sale.

We can begin by examining sales by it's basic components. A sale is composed of:

1. The prospect: This is your prospective customer. There are elaborate theories about the psychology of buyers. We choose not to add to those theories. Our experience has taught us that for one, not everyone is interested in reading those theories. Second, many sales people sell intuitively.

One simply uses ones powers of observation and experience and keeps matters simple. We don't devalue those theories. We simply believe that if one adheres to a few basics, the prospects will soon reveal if they will potentially buy or not.

2. The qualification: This the short interaction that will alert you to whether the customer will probably buy or not, and what will be necessary to bring them along. For example, if you have greeted the prospect and they show an interest in a product by asking it's price, you may (and never abandon your intuition and observation) find that they need more information to be convinced.

3. Presentation: If the qualification aspect of a sales interaction suggest that a customer is a likely prospect to buy, you can then make your sales presentation. You can briefly give any necessary information about your product, demonstrate it and relate its best features and benefits. It's is always best to get the prospect more active in the presentation. Touching is allowed here. Keep aware of the customers response. If you cannot close the sale right after the presentation. The next aspect of the transaction is usually:

4. Overcoming obstacles: At this point you have identified the prospects interest, made your sales presentation and can now identify what factors are inhibiting the customer. Perhaps the customer feels the prices you quoted are inhibitive. You must find an acceptable way to convince the customer that your prices are fair or give them some other incentive to buy. There are many ways to accomplish this. For example, if the customer thinks your price for a piece is too high, you may then counter this with a reiteration of an exceptional feature, i.e. "Well ma'am, I understand why you may feel that way, however, did you realize that the trade beads I used in this piece are from the 15th century and were in a family of

village artisans for 300 years--a treasure".

Whatever the prohibitive factor, in order to get beyond this point to a purchase point, you must work hardest and smartest. Many customers need no additional convincing. On the other hand, many customers need to be brought along completely. Keep in mind that this is the point in the interaction that most customers are lost. Be on your best behavior here.

5. Closing: If you have guided the prospects through whatever inhibited them from buying, Congratulations! You can close the sale. Don't try to rush through this, unless of course the customer is in a hurry. It is best to be polite and encouraging. If you have paid close attention to this book so far, you would have strategically placed a point of purchase item before the customer in an area he or she would be sure to see it. If you rush, you will miss the opportunity to sell that item, or even suggest any additional craft work you have available. For example: "I have gift boxes and some lovely note cards that would go great with earrings you purchased..."

Make sure you thank the customer. It is the customers who make your business possible.

8. Opening the door for follow up: Once you have closed a sale, if at all possible offer some way for the customer to do business with you again. Ask if the customer would like to sign your mailing list or give them a sales brochure, catalog or business card. Make sure to say a closing statement such as, I hope to do business with you, again, or please call me and I'd be happy to give you more information about my work. You don't have to stick with a specific script. Just be sure to inspire the customer to act on contacting your or give you information so that you can contact them, again.

Remember, the more clear and graphic the promotional material you give them is, the more likely they are to remember your product, keep your information and buy from you again. They may even refer you to others. This is why your promotional materials are so important. These materials will represent you before the customers sees you personally.

Types of Sales

Any examination of the fundamentals of selling should include a brief analysis of the basic types of sales. Our experience has shown that there are three types of sales. They include:

1. The merchandise sale: This sale is based purely on the customers desire for your merchandise. No sales pitch is really required. The customer sees the product, likes it, and buys it. A monkey could sell it to them.

2. The benefit or feature sale: This sale transaction is more involved. After the prospect has been qualified as a potential buyer, You then give your sales pitch. What makes this sale is your convincing the prospect of the benefits and features of the item. Keep in mind that benefits differ from features. Benefits is exactly what word implies, the product offers certain benefits, For example, if a person purchases a necklace made of antique beads and components, you may relay to the customer that the necklace will over the long run appreciate in value. This is a benefit, where as the antique beads are a feature of the necklace. This type of sale is only made after the prospect understands the benefits and features of the product.

3. The personality sale: This sale takes place because of how the prospect feels about you. They may enjoy your wit, charm and selling skill and buy as a gesture

of support. They may even have ulterior motives that go beyond the scope of this G-rated book. On the other hand, they may be totally turned off by your obnoxious tenacity and hard sell tactics and buy simply so you can leave them alone. That's not common in this business, fortunately. In any case, the sale is closed based primarily on your personality.

There are of course grey areas in selling. I must reiterate however, they key is to be intuitive, respectful and aware. Body language, questions the customers ask and even (though this is tricky) appearances can indicate what customers will want from you. If you keep these three sale types in mind, you will be able to analyze your sales performance better, as well as meet the needs of prospective customers better.

Selling Essentials

No understanding of selling would be complete without making mention of the essential areas of selling that make customers most comfortable. These areas are the boosters to really "making it big" in the crafts business. They include the following points:

1. Be genuine: Nothing beats an honest presentation. Don't say that your necklace was made with 4,000 year old beads when you know that they were made last year and got very dirty. Customers can often detect dishonesty. You may also be surprised to see how many knowledgeable consumers attend shows. Keep in mind the crafts circuit can be very small sometimes. If you get a reputation for being dishonest and phony, that reputation is likely to spread and you will lose all the way around.

2. Be pleasant: This means smile, have a posture of openness and interest in your customers and always extend

greetings. This kind of openness makes the customers feel welcomed and free to examine your wares.

3. Educate: Let your customers know about your merchandise. What materials did you use? What processes are involved. You don't have to use this as an opportunity to give your tell-all biography. By no means should you engage a customer so long that you ignore other customers. The point is, everyone wants a little magic in their lives. Give your customers a story. A short story. You can also use handtags on your merchandise that tells about it's origins, concept or materials. This invites inquiries. These special touches add up in dollars as you pull in sale after sale for your efforts.

4. Dress appropriately: The charm and quality of your merchandise is severely damaged if you look, smell or act like a slob. Not only should your booth and display be well groomed, so should you! You are part of the sale. Your customers buy you as much as they buy your product. Dressing appropriately doesn't particularly mean that you should wear corporate apparel. This is not expected at crafts shows. A good rule to follow is try to stick with your general image. If you sell country rag dolls, you don't have to dress like a country rag doll. The key is to tastefully suggest the image you wish to convey.

5. Greet customers as they come into and leave your booth. Of course, you may greet customers off to the side who are looking at your display and invite them in for a closer look. When a customer comes into your booth, immediately and cheerfully greet them, and then wait for a moment. This gives them time to look. Then you can ask them if there is something in specific they are looking for, if you can help them find something, or tell them some feature or benefit of what they are looking at. This should be done with whatever you observe to be the customers needs to be

in mind. When the customer leaves, make sure to thank them, whether they buy or not. If they seem like a good prospect, offer them a way to contact you later or ask them to sign your mailing list. You can even say, "keep us in mind" or "I hope to see you later in the show". Even saying, "Please tell your friends about us," is good (often customers will).

6. Go the extra mile: Try to be as accommodating as possible. Accepting checks, or credit cards if you have the means, holding merchandise for customers who have to come back (try to get a deposit) and offering whatever services will make buying from you more attractive, is always good marketing. Be creative in approaching this aspect of selling. Be aware, however, of timing. Don't spend so much time with one customer that you miss all your other customers. This is why having an assistant is so valuable. They can free you to give some customers more specialized attention.

Boothsmanship

Boothmanship can be defined as the behavior your exhibit in your booth. This of course is not limited to being in your booth literally. It implies your overall behavior at a show. Good boothmanship is vital to your success at a show. Your performance here can mean a gain or loss of many sales. Some boothmanship rules to follow are:

1. Keep yourself in order: This include regulating your stress, staying cool and calm, and pacing yourself so that you can effective serve your customers while maximizing sales. Shows are serious business but you can enjoy yourself, also. Keep the mood light and fun. Customers can sense any tension you may be feeling. Most importantly, be on your best behavior! Follow all the rules of business etiquette you know and then follow them again!

A show is not the place to be loose and offensive.

2.   Be aware of your products: This awareness includes not just knowing all about your products, but know where they are within your display or in your back up stock. This information is very helpful in helping customers decide on buying and being aware of your stock makes you more efficient overall.   It also is helpful to keep you aware of merchandise to avoid theft.

3. Know the show: If you are aware of the show, you know how to best use it to your advantage. This includes understanding traffic flow, where bathrooms and food vendors and telephones are and the overall show layout.

4. Be confident: A show is not an avenue for you to work out your insecurities. Customers being impressed by your confidence is more appealing than those same customers feeling sorry for you.

5. Treat customers equally: Every customer you have should be treated with the same level of respect. There are customers who will require more attention, but no other customers should be ignored. They, too, may have needs that require attention to close a sale. Of course, never judge and dismiss any customer by appearance only.

6. Don't smoke, sit, or eat or drink in front of your customers.   If you were a door to door salesperson, you would never do those things and get good results. Don't let your common sense lapse in a show environment.

7.   Keep conversation with your colleagues at a minimum: A show is not a party. All your attention should be kept on customers and meeting their needs. Take care of business in a business situation.

8. Be hospital: If you see that a customer looks exhausted, offer to let them sit down or allow them to put their packages under your table while they look. These little services endear you to a customer.

9. Keep your booth neat: A sloppy image is one of the worst projections you can make to customers. It puts your work in a bad light also. If you use shows to get wholesale customer, keep in mind that if at a show your booth is unkempt, a buyer is likely to feel that if they buy from you will somewhere along the lines provide them with poor quality work. It doesn't take a tremendous amount of effort to stay neat and organized. Just put things where they belong after you use them and straighten up after customers. Those things alone can keep your booth well enough to make a good impression.

10. Don't whine or complain about how the show is going: There is a saying that goes, "Never let them see you sweat". This rings true for the crafts business. Even if its five minutes till closing on the last day of the show and you haven't made any sales, keep your positive mental attitude. And by no means go complaining to other vendors. If you must complain, approach the promoter in a professional manner at another time.

11. If you have an assistant to help you, take a look at other booths and meet a few crafts people. The network is strong, and often fellow crafts people can turn you on to some very helpful information. Do not prolong this process though, and remember to collect business cards. Then, get back to your own booth, fresh with ideas and contact and make some money.

12. Don't complain about or badmouth other vendors: This is definitely a business etiquette no-no. Keep the positive energy flowing. Pettiness is best left behind at

shows.

Attracting Buyers:

One of the most important aspects of doing shows is the contacts you can make. Buyers from stores, galleries, mail order operation and art brokers are always on the look out for fresh new products. Power showing include making a impact on these buyers. In order to attract the attention of buyers, you must first try to anticipate their needs. Buyers primarily want:

1. To buy: This is the reason crafts buyers attend crafts shows. They are an eager, built in market. It's up to you to have the appeal to make the deal!

2. To supply their specific markets: Trust us when we say that buyers know who they are buying for. They study catalogs, trends, and listen carefully to the

needs of their customers. Often buyers have already studied pre-show advertising and know exactly what they want from a visit to a show. You rarely have to second guess a professional buyer, however, there are instances in which buyers are simply looking for something new to present to their market. Still, there are parameters for this kind of looking.

3. A harmonious product line: By this we mean that a buyer does not look for a such a diverse range of merchandise in one vendor that it's difficult to distinguish that the work was made by the same person. It is always a good idea to have a style that is easy to identify. Remember that the even in offering a range of product, you can have harmony, balance, and cohesiveness. This distinguishes you in the minds of buyers.

4. A range and volume of product to judge your work by: Do not try the minimalist approach in your booth and display. You don't want to overwhelm, but on the other hand, you don't want so few products that a serious buyer will brand you as an amateur with nothing to offer. Also, enough volume gives the buyer an idea of how your products show together, as well as your ability to produce quality volume.

5. The right price: Whatever your retail prices are, the smart buyer will almost always reduce that by half to figure your wholesale price range. Always keep wholesaling in mind when you price if you are going to wholesale your work. No matter what the show, the potential to find a wholesale customer exists. If your prices are high, you can say goodbye to your buyers. Make sure your products are clearly marked. If a buyer asks if you wholesale, don't be ambivalent. Buyers don't have time to play around with you. If you are going to wholesale be clear about it, and be ready to make some power moves at the show. It helps to have a wholesale price list, catalog or order form handy. Any brochures about your company are also important.

Miscellaneous Power Moves

1. Find a way in your display to highlight certain items. These items may include exclusive items, or top sellers. Use lighting, signs, special table space, placing other high interest items near it, etc. Keep your creativity flowing.

2. Have plenty of promotional material. You can even have someone at the show passing out a flyer about your work with a map to your booth. This is very effective.

3. Do something interesting: Customers love to see demonstrations or something that puts you more in an more

active stance. Try to think of things you can do that will not take too much time away from selling. This should work for you, not against you.

4. Do a promotion: Any type of sale item at your booth attracts attention and is a good marketing strategy. It pays if you announce this strategy in advance also, i.e. direct mail, the show guide or pre-show advertising. You don't have to have a bargain basement image to be effective at doing this. Most crafts buyers are not interested in a bargain basement image anyway. Crafts are mainly luxury purchases and should convey a image of luxury however subtle. Make sure your promotion is not so severe that it lessens the quality of your work in the eyes of your market. Also, be sure your promotion is clear. Good signs are helpful in this.

All of our years selling crafts in the marketplace have taught us one important lesson: common sense reigns! Courtesy, good service, excellent merchandise and creative marketing go a long way in helping you make the best out of a show. If you keep these things as your foundation, you will not fail.

CHAPTER 9

WHOLESALE AND CONSIGNMENT SELLING

In the crafts market, wholesaling represents one of the first ways to expand your business. Wholesaling your crafts is not particularly easy. There are considerations which if your are unaware of, could drain your finances, however, once the wholesale market is understood, it can be one of the most effective ways of marketing your product, providing exposure, a greater share of the general market and cash flow as well.

What is Wholesaling

There is obviously a big difference between a wholesaler and a retailer. Retailers sell to the public in small quantities and charge full retail price. Retailers either manufacture the product themselves, i.e, when you sell your products retail at a show, or they buy from wholesalers or distributors. Retailers also buy directly from manufacturers. Wholesale distributors, on the other hand, work with larger volumes, smaller margins (usually about 10%) and buy and sell at wholesale and below wholesale prices.

In the crafts business, it is surprising to note the large number of crafts people who are not only not profiting from wholesaling, but losing money as well. Wholesaling is far more involved than just selling a few of your items at half the retail price. Wholesaling is a business in and of itself.

Unless you are a very seasoned and productive crafts person, we don't recommend jumping into wholesaling right away. The challenges and frustrations are too numerous for a novice to handle effectively. Once one is firmly rooted in the fundamentals of selling in the marketplace, however, one should be ready to take on the wholesaling adventure.

Wholesale Markets

Wholesale markets are varied, but for practicality, we will stick with the basic ones. These include:

1. Galleries: Galleries are an excellent wholesale market. They offer exclusivity and usually a motivated, sophisticated market. Galleries can often sell your work at top retail price, making the deal more attractive to you overall. Do not overlook museum shops also, to sell your work. These outlets usually attract very motivated buyers.

2. Stores: Stores and shops can offer a crafts person stability in the wholesale marketplace. Usually a store that sells your work will be interested in buying from you long term and very consistently. Try to establish a good relationship with local stores and the stores that the national stores that sell your work. This can be accomplished by filling orders and delivering them on time and in good condition. This could also mean updating your line often and offering a fresh approach to your signature pieces.

3. Mail Order Operations: There are many mail order crafts catalogs as varied as the businesses that create them. Most are trade publications that will feature the work of a crafts person in a similar matter as a crafts trade show. A juring process could be involved and advertising and listing fees as well. The market however is great, as these operations can usually yield some excellent accounts. Space in these magazines is at a premium, however, and the competition is extensive.

4. Art Brokers: Art brokers are usually serious
power movers. They have extensive contacts and accounts
with large corporations. Individuals and businesses solicit
the services of art brokers in order to supply their offices
with art. Art brokers sell retail primarily, but there are
some that provide wholesale buyers with art. Keep in mind
if you work with a wholesale art broker that their fee
(usually 15 percent) will have to be factored in your sales
expenses.

Types of Wholesale Sales

Our experience shows that there are basically three
types of wholesale purchases. They are the following:

1. Direct wholesale purchases: In this type of
wholesale interaction the buyer purchases the item outright.
The payment can be in advance or deposit and 30 day net,
15 day net, or several other terms and incentives.

2. Selling on Approval: This is a relatively un
popular approach in which the buyer, rather than
purchasing up front tests the product in his retail outlet for
a limited time. This time frame could be ten days or two
weeks, even one month, but not more than sixty days. At
the end of this time period the buyer will either purchase
the entire package wholesale or pay for the items that were
sold, returning the rest of the package. This arrangement
is much like consignment selling, only the return can be
potentially higher.

If the buyer is an established wholesale customer of
yours, you can use this method to test new lines. The loss
to you is minimal and the wholesale customer risks nothing.

Consignment selling

Consignment selling works very similar to selling on approval, but rather than the store or gallery having the option of buying your products at the end of the designated time period, the agreement up front is that the owner will not buy the products at all and will take a percentage of whatever is sold. This percentage is usually about 30%, however, I've seen consignment shops and galleries that have taken percentages of up to 50%.

This situation can work well for shop owners who pay nothing for your merchandise, but for crafts people, this is more often than not, not so good. The crafts person's, merchandise is unavailable for you to sell for whatever period of time, with no possibility of the store owner purchasing it.

This kind of selling can seem very appealing to crafts people, especially beginners. Although it does offer some exposure, if you are not very well stocked, it can be more trouble than it is worth. Most of your energy should be put in marketing venues that will put cash in hand. Because the consignment deal will require no purchase on the part of the shop or gallery owner, you can be sure your products will not be sold as aggressively as product that these same owners purchase wholesale.

Another kind of problem arises as time lapses. You will have to keep checking periodically to see if your work has sold. If it does sell, you may have to then track the owner down to get paid. If you can stay positive and deal with these challenges though then consignment selling may be a good way for you to get cash flow. We still recommend, however, getting the owner to purchase wholesale.

Finding wholesale markets

If you have made the decision to wholesale, the next step is to find wholesale markets. With the interest in crafts at an all time high, there are may outlets to choose from. There are also many sources which can put you in contact with wholesale buyers. We have outlined below some of the most common.

Trade Magazines

Trade magazines for artist and crafts people, such as The Crafts Reporter, Niche, Matter and the Gift Reporter are wholesale networks in print. These publications have resources for crafters looking for wholesalers and wholesalers looking for crafters. Never overlook these publications. Even if you don't think that your work is suited for what you perceive as their market, I guarantee you almost every kind of craft work is featured in these publications.

Business Directories

There are business directories for almost every kind of business. The crafts business is no exception. The library can often provide information on where these directories are available and many times, the library will own these directories (also see the resource chapter of this book).

We suggest that you find and purchase as many as possible. Nothing that valuable to your business should not be considered as an investment into your success as a crafts person.

Trade Shows

Trade shows are wonderful opportunities for crafts people. They are an education in themselves. At crafts trade shows you have the opportunity to see the best in crafts marketing, display, boothsmanship and craftwork, as well as meet some of the most important buyers in the industry. They are worth the investment (usually fee's are very high). You can often take orders or even sell wholesale the products you have with you on the spot. Just remember that unlike retail shows, you are not there to make cash on the spot, but rather to get exposure, contacts and generate interest in your product and marketing strategies.

Trade shows are probably the best, most efficient way to begin wholesaling. Just make sure you have enough products or that you can produce enough to fill orders. If you are unable to fill orders in time, you may get a bad reputation in the business, even if you've just started wholesaling.

Retail Shows

Retail shows are primarily for retail selling, however, in many cases buyers come to these shows looking for crafts, especially from newcomers to the marketplace. We have met some of our best wholesale contact from vending at craft shows. We don't recommend that you sell any products wholesale on the spot at a retail show, unless you are at the very end of the show. This keeps your stock available for greater earnings. Do, however, have ordering information available at a retail show. Even if it is a small holiday bazaar. If you wholesale, have this information available wherever you do business. It should be as available as your business card.

Sales Representatives

Sales representatives can often get you contacts that you may not be able to get on your own. This includes wholesale contacts. A lot depends on the way you work with a sales representative. Sales representatives have to be paid. If the sales representative gets a one time finders fee (up to 30%) for a wholesale contact they give you this may work well for you. Keep in mind however, that some sales representatives require a fee every time the wholesale contact they gave you buys from you. The wholesale price you sell to your client at, plus the sales representative's fee can be prohibitive to some. Make sure you are clear on all terms before using a sales representative.

Direct Mail

If you have a good list, it is possible to get wholesale clients as a result of a direct mailing. Mailing list can be obtained from list brokers (see your yellow pages under mail services) or from your own research. You can also used cards you've collected in your business of store and gallery owners. Send a package which includes a cover letter, bio, information about your company and product, catalog, brochures, and anything else that would give a clear picture of the work that you do. Sending samples may also be a good idea (if you can afford to. This depends on your product). Photos and slides may work in lieu of samples.

You must make your presentation visually appealing and representative of the image you wish to portray. This cannot be emphasized enough.

What is important in finding wholesale markets, just as in finding retail markets, is that you use your creativity.

Wholesale Marketing Strategies

1. Before you can even begin to supply your crafts to the wholesale market you must have an adequate amount to sell. It will never be worth your while to wholesale if your work is piece mealed out at wholesale prices. We suggest that you set a wholesale purchase amount for your wares.

You can place the minimum on merchandise volume, i.e., a wholesale minimum of 1 dozen pieces, or a wholesale price rate, i.e. a minimum purchase of $150.00. Be sure to have enough of your work available for wholesalers and distributors to purchase. Be sure to be able to supply your work should other unexpected wholesale orders come available.

2. Approach prospective wholesale clients with absolute professionalism. This begins with the proper presentation. When you make your initial contact, have enough materials that represent who you are and what you do available for the prospect to examine. If your initial contact is by mail, use a cover letter, a resume, your sales literature and photos, slides or samples of your work. These formalities make a much better impression than any walk in.

After you have sent your materials, follow up in about a week to discuss any interest the buyer may have in purchasing your product and to make an appointment. When you appear for your appointment, be on your profession best behavior. Be well groomed and courteous, even if the prospect doesn't buy. Never leave scowling at a prospective customer if they don't buy immediately.

If you do decide the walk in approach, again, be well groomed and polite. No buyer is obligated to see you just because you've walked through the door. Identify yourself to whoever is available to help you and ask for the buyer or manager (often the manager and buyer are different). Always try to talk to the person who does the buying first. This saves you a lot of time and hassle from uncooperative sales people.

When you meet the buyer or manager, explain who you are and ask if you may take a few moments of their time to show them your work. Always do this. Give them your promotional materials. This should be done whether they buy or even look at your work immediately or not. Always leave an open door to do business with a prospect.

If the buyer is interested and available to look at your product line immediately, be prepared to answer any questions they may have about your product, prices, market, supply, etc. They may want to know who else you sell to in the area.

Regardless of what their final decision is, stay courteous. This is not a business to burn bridges in. Keep the door open for future business.

3. Follow up any contacts you pursue. You can do this by mail, phone, or visits. If you decide to visit, try and get an appointment. If you walk in, try to have some idea of what time and days the buyer is available, and always ask for permission to take up their time.

4. Advertise to attract wholesale buyer markets. Magazines like those listed above are excellent. The magazines Niche, Matter and The Gift Reporter cater specifically to retailers. These publications offer advertising and you are guaranteed exposure to fine wholesale markets.

You don't necessarily have to advertise with retailer magazines. Many magazines, such as Ornament, have large readerships of galleries and stores. Keep open for possibilities by studying adds, magazines and trade journals that may be read by companies interested in crafts.

5. Offer an incentive to wholesale buyers. This could be done by offering a discount on greater volume (a graduated pricing schedule) which would encourage buyers to purchase more at a time.

6.   Try special promotions for your wholesale prospects or customers. Offer free samples or extra products if ordered by a certain deadline.   There are many possibilities. Study basic marketing techniques and see if you can find any strategies you could use for your crafts business. By all means, study and talk to seasoned crafts people and find their marketing strategies.

7. Make sure your products or buyer friendly. Buyers who are not able to handle your products easily will be put off. Make your work as direct and simple to deal with as possible, both for wholesale buyers and general consumers.

8. Be creative in collecting names. Just as business exhibitors offer drawings for a free (whatever), you can offer a drawing for a piece of your work at a trade show. You can have a box or bowl in which businesses can drop their cards or use a small ballot for them to fill out. This can get you thousands of names of business interested enough in your product to fill out a thousands of dollars worth of sales at a later date.

Finally, when considering wholesaling, remember that you make your money by retailers buying in volume what you can quickly (with quality produce). If production is to slow, you lose. If wholesale clients buy to little, you lose.

You can be successful at wholesaling, but is important to understand that wholesaling your crafts is much more involved than retailing them, and the payoff is not as readily available. There is far more work involved also.

It is vital that you stay focused and aware of your expenses, production cost, selling expenses, etc. (see chapter 4. This is one area in the crafts business that can cost much more if you are not meticulous.

With all that said, consider this. If you have seen a crafts person's work that you admire in a store or gallery, and you know that person to be very successful, have hope. Someone is doing it well. So, eventually, can you.

CONCLUSION

In the process of writing this book, we were reminded of so many wonderful, funny, expensive and crazy experiences as we worked to build our crafts business. What was most impressive to us, is the fact that there are so many more resources and opportunities available than when we began.

Crafts businesses can make millionaires today. We know people who have accomplished this. That is not to say that it is easy. The crafts business is not a get rich quick scheme. If you are interested in a hustle, there are far easier hustles than marketing and selling your crafts, but if you wish to build a livelihood on your own creativity, the crafts business has much to offer you.

We did not aspire to make this book the only resource you will ever need, although for the very industrious, it just may well be. We had no books like this when we began, though we do recommend that you read as much as possible about the business. The point we are trying to make is that little can be much in this business, and with this book, some hard work and a lot of creativity you can be well on your way.

We purposely made the book easy to understand, using as little jargon and complex ideas as possible. Our intent was to make a book that any crafts person, including those who will be crafts people in the future, will read this book and use it as a catalyst to greater things.

In the following appendixes, we have provided

resources that can take your crafts business as far as your dreams dictate. It is our sincere desire that anyone who has a strong enough will to do so, will find the crafts business, a vehicle for success, wealth and self-reliance.

May anyone who reads this book make it, and MAKE IT BIG!

APPENDIX I

GENERAL BUSINESS RESOURCES

Every person embarking upon a business should have a basic understanding of the primary principles all businesses are based on. This gives a firm foundation to build any venture on.

The following general business resources include publications, government agencies and miscellaneous business helps. Although these resources are not specifically for crafts business, the information is very beneficial for crafts people and can be tailored to meet any specific business needs.

Books

Bandele's Annual Small Business Guide
to African-American Events
Bandele Publications
P.O. Box 21540
Washington, D.C.20009
(301)779-7730

The Noble Art of Vending
By Gabriel Bandele
Bandele Publications
P.O. Box 21540
Washington, D.C. 20009

Black Economics
Solutions for Economic and Community Empowerment
by Jawanza Kunjufu
African American Images
Chicago, IL

Black Folks Guide To Business Success
by George Subira
Very Serious Business
Newark, N.J

Your Small Business Made Simple
by Richard Gallagher, D.B.A
A Made Simple Book
Doubleday Books
New York

Small-Time Operator
How to Start Your Own Small Business, Keep Your Books,
Pay Your Taxes, and Stay Out of Trouble
by Bernard Kamoroff, C.P.A.
Bell Springs Publishing
P.O. Box 640
Laytonville, CA 95454

Homebased Businesses
by Beverly Nuerer Feldman, Ed.D.
Fawcett Crest
New York

Working From Home
by Paul and Sarah Edwards
Jeremy P. Tarcher, Inc.
Los Angeles

Magazines

Black Enterprise
130 Fifth Avenue
New York, N.Y. 10011
(202)242-8000

Home Office Computing
730 Broadway
New York, N.Y. 10003

Government Agencies

Department of Commerce
14th and Constitution Avenue, N.W.
Washington, D.C. 20233
(202)447-4572

Minority Business Development Agency
This national network of business
assistance centers offers various aids and resources
for minority businesses. Call the Communications
Division at (202)377-2414 to get referals to the
appropriate unit within the agency.

Office of Business Liason
(202)377-3176-This agency also makes referrals to
appropriate
agencies as well as publishes a free Business Services
directory,
available by request.

Government Printing Office
Order and Information Desk (202)783-3228
This agency sells and distributes many useful government publications.

Small Business Administration
1111 18th Street, N.W., 6th Floor
Washington, D.C. 20036
This agency provides financial assistance, business development helps, procurement assistance and advocacy programs. There arelocal chapters of the SBA nationwide.

APPENDIX II

CRAFTS BUSINESS RESOURCES

The most resourceful craftsperson, is the craftsperson with the most resources. The following resources are specifically related to the crafts business and include a full range of products and services from publications to supplies and equipment.

Utilizing these resources can also lead you to other resources, giving you the opportunity express your full range of capabilities.

Crafts Business Publications

Directory of African-American Prints, Posters, and Crafts Dealers
by James Lewis
David Alake Bakari Lewis Publishing
1553 Woodward Avenue #202
Box 711
Detroit, Michigan 48226

African American Products Catalog
P.O. Box 6890
108 North Magnolia Avenue
Suite 316
Ocala, Florida 32678
(904)629-1664

Black Satin Collectibles Catalog:
An Afrocentric Marketplace
601 Pennsylvania Avenue.
Suite 700, North Building
Washington, D.C. 20004
(202)554-5177

You Can Make Money From Your Arts and Crafts:
The Arts and Crafts
by Steve and Cindy Long
Mark Publishing - Be Your Own Boss Series
15 Camp Evers Lane
Scotts Valley, CA 95066
1-800-622-7372

Sell What You Make:
The Business of Marketing Crafts
by Paul Gerhards
Stockpole Books
Cameron Kelker Streets
P.O. 1831
Harrisburg, PA 17105

Ornament
Ornament, Inc.
1221 S. La Cienega
Los Angeles, CA 90035
(213)652-9914

Lapidary Journal
P.O. Box 1100
Devon, PA 19333-0905
(215)293-1112

The Crafts Report
700 Orange Street
Wilmington, DE 19899

Matter
GLM Publications, a division of
George Little Management, Inc.
215 Lexington Avenue, Suite 1901
New York, NY 10016

GR (Gift Reporter)
215 Lexington Ave., 19th Floor
New York, NY 10016

Lifestyle Crafts Buyers Resource Directory
2164 Riverside Drive
Columbus, Ohio 43221

Niche
c/o The Rosen Agency
3000 Chestnut Street, Ste. 300
Baltimore, MD 21211
(410)889-2933

Trade Shows and Promoters

International Fashion Boutique Show
Corporate Headquarters
100 Wells Avenue
P.O. Box 9105
Newton, MA 02159
(617)964-5100

George Little Management, Inc.
Registration Services
215 Lexington Avenue
New York, NY 10016-6023
(800)272-SHOW, (212)686-6070

Art Buyers Caravan
c/o Decor Magazine
330 North Fourth Street
St. Louis, MO 63102

International Gem and Jewelry Show, Inc.
4601 North Park Avenue
Chevy Chase, MD 20815

American Crafts Enterprises, Inc.
P.O. Box 10, 256 Main Street
New Paltz, NY 12561
(800)836-3470

Retail Show Resources

Bandele's Annual Small Business Guide to
African-American Events
Bandele Publications
P.O. Box 21540
Washington, D.C. 20009
(301)779-7530

Organizations

African Greeting Card Collective
P.O. Box 90485
Washington, D.C. 20090-0485
1-800-927-0429

American Crafts Retailer Association (ACRA)
1838 East Second Street
Scotch Plains, NJ 07076
(201)322-6207

APPENDIX III

EQUIPMENT RESOURCES

Sky Cap Canopy Company
37 West 19th Street
New York, NY 10011
(212)691-0175

Easy Up Canopy Products
4815 Trousdale Drive
Nashville, TN 37220

KD Kanopy, Inc.
5758 Lamar Street
Arvada, CO 80002

Tri-Conn, Inc.
143 Golden Hill St.
P.O. Box 190
Bridgeport, CT 06601 (203)334-7816

The Supply Source
8805 N. Main Street
Dayton, Ohio 45415

Elaine Martin, Inc.
P.O. Box 261
Highwood, IL 60040